India : Redeeming the Economic Pledge

BIBEK DEBROY is Director of the Rajiv Gandhi Institute for Contemporary Studies, Rajiv Gandhi Foundation, New Delhi. He is a professional economist and was educated in Presidency College (Calcutta), Delhi School of Economics and Trinity College (Cambridge). He has worked at Presidency College (Calcutta), Gokhale Institute of Politics and Economics (Pune), Indian Institute of Foreign Trade (Delhi), National Council of Applied Economic Research (Delhi) and as Consultant, Department of Economic Affairs, Ministry of Finance, Government of India. He was also the Director for a project known as LARGE, set up by the Ministry of Finance and UNDP to examine legal reforms. He is the author and editor of several books, papers and popular articles and is also Consulting Editor with Financial Express. Bibek Debroy's special interests are international trade (in particular the WTO), law reform and the political economy of liberalization in India. He has been listed in many biographies and has been a member of several government committees.

India : Redeeming the Economic Pledge

BIBEK DEBROY

ACADEMIC FOUNDATION

NEW DELHI

Published in 2004 by
ACADEMIC FOUNDATION
4772-73 / 23 Bharat Ram Road,
(23 Ansari Road), Darya Ganj,
New Delhi - 110 002. INDIA.

Phones : 23245001, 02, 03, 04.
Fax : 011-23245005
e-mail : academic@vsnl.com
www : academicfoundation.com

India : Redeeming the Economic Pledge
by Bibek Debroy
ISBN 81-7188-348-6

Printed and bound in India.

For

Dipavali

CONTENTS

Foreword

IN the 1990s, the Indian economy has grown fairly rapidly. In fact, it is one of the fastest growing economies in the world. Despite our impressive attainments since Independence, India has tended to fall behind, particularly in comparison with other dynamic economies of Asia. To catch up with them as well as to fulfill our promise, we need to take the growth rate to even higher levels.

To ensure such movement to a higher growth trajectory that is sustained over a long period of time, we need more reforms and their energetic implementation. There is reasonable consensus among economists about what this package of second-generation reforms needs to be. I have elsewhere categorized these reforms into macro, meso and micro reforms. If these reforms are not implemented and it continues to be business as usual, we will trundle along and not be able to break out of the threat of India's diminishing role in the world economy. However, if reforms are implemented, there is no reason why India should not exhibit real national income growth rates of 8% or 9% over the next twenty years or so. To exit from the gravitational pull of poverty, we need the exit velocity of high growth.

The first flush of reforms in 1991 was crisis-driven. These measures also concerned liberalization in the external sector. Such reforms are easier than reforms in the domestic economy. The second-generation reforms therefore need to be consensus-driven. They cannot be forcibly thrust down and one encounters what is often called the political economy of reforms problem. But provided information is disseminated and debate encouraged, there is no reason why a consensus cannot be generated.

Debate and consensus require dissemination of information as a prerequisite. And this communication cannot always be directed at the professional economist. There is a need to communicate to a broader audience. This task cannot be left to the government alone. Each of us who believes in reforms has this responsibility. I am glad that at least one – who is also one of India's outstanding economists – has decided to write a popular book on reforms. The style is lucid and reader friendly and this is a book that ordinary interested people should enjoy reading. Prof. Debroy has done seminal work in studying the interface between economics and law and this book covers his pioneering contribution in this important area.

For me, in this book, there is a remarkable coincidence ! In a recently delivered lecture on India's economic reforms, I ended with the following sentence : "By the year 2020, in terms of Human Development Index, we can be among the first twenty and thus fulfill that long awaited promise which Jawaharlal Nehru so eloquently described as our tryst with destiny." I have no idea whether Bibek Debroy was sub-consciously influenced by this sentence. But coincidence is that this book begins and ends with the tryst with destiny speech and also has an allusion to the speech in the title.

Not every reform area is equally covered. But that is a question of emphasis and one's preferences. Given the author's areas of interest, there is an understandable bias towards trade and law, but I hope that there will be future books from him covering equally important issues such as sustainable development, employment generation, regional equity and technological progress. All of us will benefit from his undoubtedly innovative perspectives to these vital issues.

I thoroughly enjoyed reading this book and so should you.

Vijay Kelkar

New Delhi,
January, 2004.

Preface

THERE are several books on the Indian economy. Arguably, the 1990s stimulated greater interest in the Indian economy and the number of books has also correspondingly proliferated. Each such book proclaims that it will be of great interest to students, researchers, teachers, policy-makers, lay people, everyone under the sun. I have no such hallowed intention, nor such an overwhelming target audience.

It is best to set out one's biases clearly. I believe the Indian economy has under-performed. I believe economic reforms are necessary to push India to a higher growth trajectory. I believe the present system is anti-poor and pro-rich and *ipso facto*, any reforms will be pro-poor and anti-rich. And I also happen to think that most sensible economists hold similar points of view, although there can be debates about the definition of reforms and their appropriate sequencing. This is a book about reforms. It is a book that argues for reforms. But I have no desire to address the audience of researchers, teachers, fellow economists or policy-makers. They know, or should know, all this.

There is an argument that the message of reforms has not been sold to Indian citizens. Reforms have been thrust down from top, in ad hoc fashion. The bottom-up groundswell of support hasn't happened and that explains why political parties believe there are no votes to be obtained through a reform message. This thus explains the political economy of resistance. If the reform message has to be sold, that can't be done solely through the pink papers. Nor through the English language press.

I have written, and continue to write, for the pink papers. I have written, and continue to write, for the English language press. But I also write for the vernacular press. I have written a series of columns for *Ananda Bazar Patrika* in Bengali. I have also written a series of columns for *Andhra Jyoti* in Telegu. (The Telegu version was written in English and translated by someone else). These two sets of columns set out the arguments for reform. This book is based on those columns. These columns haven't quite appeared in English. But nor is this English language rendition an exact reproduction of what appeared in Bengali and Telegu. The content is similar, but not identical. And the form does vary a bit from the Bengali and Telegu versions.

Having sought to target the vernacular, why get back to English ? Because there is a lay public audience there as well. At least, the publisher, Academic Foundation, thinks so. And surely, publishers know markets far better than authors do. That explains this book. Not every reform area has been covered. That would be too much to expect. There are undoubtedly errors of omission, inevitable thanks to a columnist's personal preferences and biases. For instance, there is much more on international trade and law, relatively speaking. But hopefully, there aren't errors of commission. And taken collectively, this book may succeed in communicating to a broader audience why most economists believe that reforms are necessary. If even a little bit of that objective is attained, the effort will have been worthwhile.

Authors of most books have numerous debts they wish to acknowledge. I have very few, because I have so freely drawn upon the research work of my fellow economists, often without any acknowledgement. Nevertheless, I do have six. First, I must thank *Ananda Bazar Patrika* and *Andhra Jyoti* for having asked me to write the respective Bengali and Telegu columns. These columns eventually made the present book possible. Second, I must thank the readers of those columns. Hate mail, and the relatively rarer, fan mail helped improve subsequent columns. Third, I must thank the entire Kapila family for their enthusiasm and their belief that there was a reasonable book in this content. Without this belief, the book wouldn't have materialized. Fourth, I must thank Laveesh Bhandari, my co-author in several inter-State, inter-district and assorted other studies and not just for providing the graphs. He was the non-anonymous referee and his enthusiasm was infectious. Laveesh also put me in touch with my fifth creditor. Thus, fifth, I must thank Anoop Kamath, who worked wonders with his cartoons of the new common man. Sixth, the Foreword by Vijay Kelkar gives the book academic respectability and these words of praise will hopefully not raise as many hackles as the Kelkar Task Force's recommendations did.

Finally, this book is for Dipavali. Most authors feel compelled to dedicate their first book to their spouse. Across several books, perhaps inexplicably, I have never done this. All kinds of relatively distant people have instead figured in dedications. Probably because I felt those books were boring. Too specialized. I think this book is an exception. I think this book is interesting. And after all, the year of publication does coincide with our twenty-fifth wedding anniversary.

Bibek Debroy

New Delhi,
January, 2004.

1

Where Do We Stand?

I am an economist and what interests me is the Indian economy. And the Indian economy now is about economic reforms. So that's what this book will focus on, different aspects of reforms. Reforms have been around for more than a decade. But there is still confusion in several people's minds about why liberalization is at all necessary.

Why are reforms necessary? Let's begin at the beginning. For me, the beginning is a quote.

"Long years ago, we made a tryst with destiny, and now the time comes when we shall redeem our pledge, not wholly or in full measure, but very substantially. At the stroke of the midnight hour, when the world sleeps, India will awake to life and freedom."

As everyone knows, this is a familiar quote. I wasn't born in 1947. I have absolutely no idea of what it felt like to be born in a country that wasn't Independent. I have no direct means of knowing or feeling what economic conditions in India were like then. But there are people alive who listened to that speech at the stroke of midnight on 14th/15th August. They must have felt inspired. The blood that coursed through their veins must have felt different. They must have dreamt of a dream that would finally become successful. Independent India would occupy her rightful place under the sun.

More than fifty years have passed since that speech. More than fifty-six if you want to be precise. We have not only celebrated fifty years of Independence. We have also celebrated fifty years of our Constitution, a Constitution that entered into force in 1950. We often forget the Preamble to our Constitution. Here is what it says. "We the people of India... do hereby adopt, enact and give to ourselves this Constitution." Notice, as Indian citizens, we gave ourselves this Constitution. No one else gave it to us. According to the Constitution, there are three main organs of government – the Legislative, the Executive and the Judiciary. Our lives are determined and influenced by these three organs of State. However, India or the Indian economy has not been created to serve these three organs of government. The Indian economy is meant to serve the interests and well being of India's citizens. That's the reason we gave ourselves this Constitution. The three organs of State are meant to be instruments. They are not the ends.

After fifty-six years of Independence, what is the state of the Indian economy? What is the state of India's citizens?

The United Nations Development Programme (UNDP) is part of the UN system. Every year, since 1990, the UNDP has brought out a document known as the Human Development Report (HDR). This is a cross-country documentation of human development and human deprivation. The last HDR we have is for the year 2003. That means the document was published in the year 2003. There is always a time lag in collecting or processing data. Therefore, data used in the HDR for 2003 are usually for the year 2001.

India is invariably described as a poor country. There are different ways of deciding whether a country is rich or poor. Different variables can be used for the judgment. However, a standard variable used is called per capita national income or per capita income. Divide national income by population and you get per capita income. This gives an average idea about how rich or poor the citizen of a particular country is. Of course, per capita income is not the only possible indicator. But it is certainly a major one. Naturally, the Indian per capita income will be in Indian rupees. That can't immediately be compared with the per capita income of someone who lives in Britain, since that per capita income is expressed in pounds. There must be a common unit of measurement, so that comparisons become possible.

Whether we like it or not, the US economy is a powerful one. Therefore, the US dollar has come to be the common denominator according to which per capita incomes of different countries are expressed. The Indian per capita income is in rupees. We need to convert that into dollars. That is done using the exchange rate, for example, 45.5 rupees to 1 US dollar.

The World Bank is cursed in many parts of the world. So people don't have to be told that there is an organization known as the World Bank. Strictly speaking, this organization is formally called the International Bank for Reconstruction and Development (IBRD). However, the name World Bank is more common. The World Bank does many things. One of the minor things it does is to generate the per capita incomes of different countries of the world, expressed in US dollars. Every year, the World Bank brings out a document known as World Development Indicators. You'll find the per capita incomes of different countries stated there. There is also a slimmer volume known as the World Bank Atlas. That also gives per capita incomes. This method of using official exchange rates to convert per capita income in rupees into per capita income in US dollars is therefore known as the Atlas method. When UNDP gives India's per capita income, it doesn't generate these figures itself. It uses data from the World Bank.

Let's return to the HDR for 2003. What was India's per capita income in 2001? You'll get a figure of 462 US dollars. Today, in 2003, it has of course crossed 500 US dollars. But cross-country figures are available with a time lag. So let's use 462 dollars. Is that high or low? Is that rich or poor? Difficult to answer, because many things in life are relative. We need to know how other countries in the world are doing. In 1999, the World Bank worked out per capita incomes for 206 countries in the world. Data are sometimes not available for some countries. In this ranking of 206 countries, India's rank was 162nd, judged by per capita income. Rank number 161st was occupied by Haiti and Haiti's per capita income was 10 dollars more than ours. Rank number 163rd was occupied by Nicaragua and Nicaragua's per capita income was 20 dollars less than ours.

Think about it. Is this the kind of tryst with destiny we want? Wedged in between Haiti and Nicaragua?

Reason for Dissatisfaction

All of us, as Indian citizens, have reasons to be dissatisfied with the state of the Indian economy. We are stuck with a per capita income of 500 US dollars. Switzerland, among the world's richest economies, has a per capita income of 38,350 US dollars.

There is of course a point that needs to be made about per capita income. Our per capita income is in Indian rupees. To make international comparisons, we need to convert that into US dollars. So an exchange rate is needed. When the World Bank publishes per capita income figures, it uses official exchange rates. Say, 45.5 rupees against 1 US dollar. But the point is the following. For 45.5 rupees, I can buy many more goods (or services) in India than I can buy for 1 US dollar in the United States. Therefore, official exchange rates don't really capture the purchasing power of a currency. Economists have accordingly thought of purchasing power parity (PPP) exchange rates and these are produced by IMF (International Monetary Fund) and used by everyone else. For example, a PPP exchange rate will be around 10 rupees to 1 US dollar rather than 45.5 rupees to 1 US dollar. If everything is freely tradable, prices across the world should be the same. But everything is not freely tradable. There are restrictions on free trade in goods and most services cannot be traded. Services cost relatively less in developing countries and relatively more in developed countries. Because of this, PPP transformations tend to relatively push up per capita incomes of developing countries and push down those of developed countries.

A crude example of PPP is what you will find reported in "The Economist" magazine. This uses the price of a McDonald hamburger (a reasonably standardized product) in different countries to work out what the PPP exchange rate should be. If we use PPP, we find that India's per capita income (reported in Human Development Report 2003) is 2840 US dollars. That is certainly an improvement on 500 US dollars. But is no great reason for celebration. I mentioned earlier that if you use conventional or official exchange rates, India's rank in per capita income is 162nd out of 206 countries. If you use PPP, India's rank becomes 153rd out of 206 countries. 153rd should be no cause for celebration.

A relative comparison is not the only way to judge whether a country is rich or poor. Economists have thought of a notion known as the poverty line. To physically survive, every human being needs a certain minimum number of calories. Understandably, this calorie requirement will depend on whether I am a male or a female, whether I am an adult or a child, whether I live in rural areas or in urban areas and on my occupation. Having allowed for such differences, one can work out the minimum monthly expenditure that will be required for me to obtain these calories. That's the essential idea of a poverty line. Of course, food is not everything. So one can add some extra expenditure to cover costs of non-food necessities. The percentage of population below the poverty line (BPL) is known as the poverty ratio or the head count ratio. Per capita income gives us some idea about the state of the average Indian citizen. The poverty line tells us what percentage of the population is poor. For example, a high per capita income may simultaneously have high poverty, because the income is unevenly distributed.

To compute poverty ratios, one needs data on household income. Data on household income are collected by an organization known as NCAER (National Council of Applied Economic Research). You can't ask everyone in the country about income data. Hence, data are collected through samples rather than complete enumeration. If the sampling is done properly and if sample sizes are large enough, the sample should provide a reasonable idea about the complete population. It is generally believed that NCAER samples are not large enough. It is also believed that data on income tend to be unreliable. So although

NCAER sources can be used to compute poverty ratios, that is not what is usually done.

There is also an organization known as NSS (National Sample Survey). NSS collects data on expenditure, not income. Unfortunately, NSS samples are not conducted every year. On an average, the large sample surveys of the NSS are conducted once every five years. In between, there are thin samples with smaller sample sizes. Because the sample sizes of thin samples are small, they are not very reliable. To calculate poverty ratios, one should use the large samples. The last year for which we have large sample data from the NSS is 1999-2000. There has been some debate about the reliability of this data. I will come to that later. For the moment, using NSS data on expenditure, Planning Commission computes poverty ratios and we know that in 1999-2000, 26 per cent of the Indian population was poor. 26 per cent of the Indian population is larger than the populations of most countries in the world. Surely, this cannot be an acceptable tryst with destiny.

The poverty line I have talked about so far is called the national poverty line. This is internal to India. Internationally, a poverty line of 1 US dollar per day is also used. This figure of around 1 US dollar is at 1993 prices and for subsequent years, it has to be scaled upwards to take care of inflation. Using this poverty line, we find 34.7 per cent of the Indian population is below the poverty line. Here is a list of countries that do worse than us according to this criterion – Nicaragua, Namibia, Ghana, Lesotho, Bangladesh, Nepal, Zimbabwe, Uganda, Madagascar, Gambia, Nigeria, Rwanda, Malawi, Zambia, Central African Republic, Ethiopia, Mozambique, Burundi, Mali, Burkina Faso, Niger and Sierra Leone. Change comes from dissatisfaction. And I want to make the point that there is a lot for us to be dissatisfied with.

You might legitimately argue that income isn't everything. Per capita income may be one indicator, but we should look at other indicators also. Absolutely right. It is because per capita income doesn't reveal everything that economists have thought of physical quality of life indicators. These are things like infant mortality, life expectancy or literacy. Human Development Reports or HDRs compute an index of human development, known as the Human Development Index (HDI). How India performs on the HDI will be something we will take up later. But let me forewarn you, India does pretty badly on that also.

2

Development and Deprivation – 154 Years

IN the last chapter, I referred to UNDP's Human Development Report (HDR) and the human development index (HDI). HDI is based on three indicators of development – first, life expectancy at birth (a measure of health outcomes), second, PPP (purchasing power parity) per capita income, and third, literacy and gross enrolment ratio (a measure of education outcomes). These three are aggregated, with appropriate weights, to obtain the HDI. The maximum possible value of HDI is 1 and the minimum possible value is 0.00.

If a country has a HDI value of more than 0.800 it is classified as belonging to the high human development category. If a country has a HDI value that is between 0.500 and 0.800, it is classified as belonging to the medium human development category. Finally, if a country has a HDI value less than 0.500, it is classified as belonging to the low human development category. According to HDR, India has a HDI value of 0.590. India is just behind Morocco and just ahead of Vanuatu. Among 175 countries that are classified on the basis of HDI, India's rank is 127th. Norway leads the table and Norway's HDI value is 0.944. You might argue that Norway is a developed country. But a country like Sri Lanka has a HDI value of 0.730. More than 56 years after Independence, why should we be satisfied with a rank of 127th? Instead, as citizens of Independent India, we should feel angry.

HDI is based on some indicators of development. It doesn't include everything. Consider some other figures given in HDR, not used for computing HDI. 15.3 per cent of those born in India will not survive till the age of 40. Forty seven per cent of children under five years of age are under-weight. Only 28 per cent of the Indian population has access to adequate sanitation facilities. Twenty four per cent of the population is under-nourished. The infant mortality rate is 67 per thousand live births. The under-five mortality rate is 93 per thousand live births.

I have quoted from Jawaharlal Nehru's "Tryst with Destiny" speech earlier. Let me quote once again, "At the stroke of the midnight hour, when the world sleeps". This sounded nice, but wasn't quite accurate, was it? At the stroke of the midnight hour in India, the rest of the world wasn't asleep. When it was twelve in the night in India, it was day in most parts of the world. The rest of the world wasn't asleep. The rest of the world was awake. And there is a sad imagery there. Compared to what the rest of the world has been able to achieve, we are the ones who have been sleeping. Let me give you an example. Not from developed countries, but from a developing one. In 1960, India's per capita income was 73 US dollars, the figure for Thailand was 92. Comparisons with Thailand were possible. In 1973, India's per capita income was 120 US dollars, Thailand's was 270. Comparisons were becoming difficult. In 1999, India's per capita income was 450 US dollars, Thailand's was 1960. Comparisons were impossible. That's the reason we should feel dissatisfied. Without dissatisfaction, as I have said earlier, there is no movement for change.

There is no dearth of text-books on the Indian economy. Pick up any such text-book, used in a school or a college and look up what it has to say when it describes the Indian economy. I am prepared to bet that the textbook will say India is a developing economy. That's what we studied also, India is a developing economy. Our teachers taught us that the world is divided into two groups. There are rich countries in the world, the developed economies. Those are the haves of the world. But also in the world, there are developing economies. Those are the poor countries, the have-nots of the world. The developing economies will have to catch up with the developed countries and that will take hundreds of years. A few years ago, IMF (International Monetary Fund) brought out a table where it asked a very simple question. If you extrapolate present trends, how many years will it take a country like India to halve the gap in per capita incomes that exists between India today and the developed countries today? Notice, not eliminate the gap, but only halve it. Notice, developed countries will also grow. But the question is about halving the gap with today's per capita income, not their future income. The answer to IMF's question should surprise you, because the answer is 154 years. We have only waited for 56 years. There's another 98 years to go.

Text-books maintain this dichotomy between developed countries and developing ones. That is the thrust of developmental economics. Developing countries will have to catch up with developed economies and that will take hundreds of years. It will take generations. This entire approach to developmental economics has changed in the period following World War II. Country after country has demonstrated that you don't have to wait for hundreds of years or generations. Change can be brought about in 20 or 30 years. In a way, this altered perception started with Japan. From Japan, it spilled over into Hong Kong, South Korea, Taiwan and Singapore. From there, it spilled over into Indonesia, Malaysia and Thailand. And from there, it spilled over into China. Generally speaking, this entire region can be described as South-East Asia or East Asia. If this region didn't have to wait for 154 years, why do we have to wait that long? Marxists still think of the world as divided into a centre and a periphery. The centre is the developed world. The periphery is formed by the colonies, the developing world. The centre exploits the periphery. Before it was in some sense unified with China, Hong Kong was Britain's colony, wasn't it? Britain was the centre and Hong Kong belonged to the periphery. The centre should be richer than the periphery. You may not know that Hong Kong's per capita income is 24,850 US dollars. And Britain's per capita income is 24,160 US dollars. So much for centre-periphery.

Centre-periphery relations have gone haywire. But you won't find this described in usual Economics text-books. Economics text-books don't usually talk about East Asia. Their view of the world ends with World War II. So they still discuss the economic histories of the former Soviet Union, United States, Japan and Great Britain. It's not very surprising that we therefore have a very muddled view of the world.

Ethnocentricity

There is a word known as ethnocentricity. Ethnocentricity essentially means that I regard my country as the centre of the universe. Hence, I deduce that my country is different. It cannot be compared to any other country in the world. Every large country exhibits an element of ethnocentricity, the United States, China, India. So if comparisons are made with East Asian countries like Hong Kong, South Korea, Taiwan or Singapore, the reaction will be you can't compare India with these countries. These are small countries. India being a large country is different. You can't make comparisons with Indonesia either. Remember that Indonesia is a large country. You can't make comparisons with another large country like China. The Chinese don't have democracy. So how can you make comparisons with China? However, if all these other countries are doing better than we are, surely we should ask whether India is indeed different. And whether we made a mistake in terms of the economic policies followed.

Why do I keep harping about East Asia? India is a poor country, with a per capita income of 450 or 500 US dollars, depending on the year. You can't compare India with the richest countries of the world, countries that have per capita incomes close to 50,000 dollars a year. Those are developed countries. India should be compared to other developing countries. Fair enough. The East Asian economies are developing countries. Which of these shall we have comparisons with? Compared to India's per capita income of 462 US dollars in 2001, here are the per capita incomes of some of these countries – Singapore (20,733), Hong Kong (24,074), South Korea (8,917), Malaysia (3,699), Thailand (1,874), China (911) and Indonesia (695). With the exception of Indonesia, we don't belong in the same league at all. But these are per capita incomes using official exchange rates. And I argued that PPP (purchasing power parity) is better. Fine. Let's use PPP. In 2001, using PPP, India's per capita income was 2,840 US dollars. Here are the PPP per capita incomes of some of these countries – Singapore (22,680), Hong Kong (24,850), South Korea (15,090), Malaysia (8,750), Thailand (6,400), China (4,020) and Indonesia (2,940). Again, with the exception of Indonesia, there is no comparison at all.

So this dichotomy between developed and developing countries doesn't make a great deal of sense. What is a developing country? In the 1960s, there was indeed a definition of a developing country. A developing country was a country that had a per capita income that was 25 per cent or less than the per capita income of the United States. I said earlier that the World Bank gives us figures on per capita incomes of different countries. But the World Bank no longer uses words like developed or developing countries. Instead, you will find expressions like high-income countries, low-income countries and so on. It is of course true that in the United Nations system, there is still a definition of a developing country, categorized not only in terms of per capita income, but also variables like the diversification of the economy. The point is that developing economies are extremely heterogeneous now, much more than was the case in the 1950s. And other developing economies have demonstrated that it is possible to grow extremely fast and catch up with developed countries.

Per capita income is only one possible indicator of development and as I have mentioned earlier, it is not the only possible indicator. Take life expectancy. India's is 62.9 years, according to HDR. (This is a 1999 figure). With the exception of two countries, each of the countries I have mentioned has a life expectancy more than 70 years. The two exceptions are Thailand with 69.9 years and Indonesia with 65.8 years. India's literacy rate is 58.0 per cent. Each of these countries has a literacy rate more than 85 per cent. India's infant mortality rate per thousand is 67. Only two of the countries I have mentioned have infant mortality rates more than 30 per thousand and these are China with a figure of 31 and Indonesia with a figure of 33. As I have said, we don't belong in the same league.

And as I have also said, we should be intensely dissatisfied with this tryst with destiny. Why shouldn't the life expectancy in India be 70 years? Why shouldn't the literacy rate be 85 per cent? Why shouldn't the infant mortality rate be less than 35?

The issue of India being a poor country keeps cropping up. Explain a very simple thing. If national income doesn't grow, how will poverty be eliminated? As long as national income doesn't increase, no matter how many re-distributive policies we have, they will only amount to redistribution of poverty, not of wealth. The size of the cake has to increase. This doesn't mean that growth in national income is sufficient to eliminate poverty. But it is certainly necessary.

Forget the decade of the 1990s for the moment. Our track record of increases in real national income hasn't been particularly impressive. We got an average growth of 3.7 per cent during the First Plan (1951-56), 4.2 per cent during the Second Plan (1956-61), 2.8 per cent during the Third Plan (1961-66), 3.4 per cent during the Fourth Plan (1969-74), 5.0 per cent during the Fifth Plan (1974-79), 5.5 per cent during the Sixth Plan (1980-85) and 5.8 per cent during the Seventh Plan (1985-90). Take away the rate of population growth and the real growth in per capita income was an average of 1.8 per cent during the First Plan (1951-56), 2.0 per cent during the Second Plan (1956-61), 0.2 per cent during the Third Plan (1961-66), 1.0 per cent during the Fourth Plan (1969-74), 2.7 per cent during the Fifth Plan (1974-79), 3.2 per cent during the Sixth Plan (1980-85) and 3.6 per cent during the Seventh Plan (1985-90). There is a break in what I have reported, because we had a break in five-year plans from 1966 to 1969 and again from 1990 to 1992.

What do you notice? You notice that a period lasted till the middle of the 1970s. The average annual rate of growth was 3.5 per cent, the so-called Hindu rate of growth. This was a phrase coined by the late Professor Raj Krishna. He suggested tongue in cheek that there was something intrinsically Hindu about this rate of growth of 3.5 per cent, as a result of which the Indian economy never seemed to do better. Till the middle of the 1970s, this Hindu rate didn't change. We will continue with this argument later.

3

Growth and Poverty

SINCE 1947, if one judges by real GDP (gross domestic product) growth, the Indian economic transition can be divided into three stages. The first stage lasted till the mid-1970s and annual average GDP growth didn't cross 3.5 per cent, the so-called Hindu rate of growth. The second stage lasted from the late 1970s to the 1980s, when the annual average GDP growth increased to 5 per cent in the second half of the 1970s and 5.5 per cent in the 1980s. Perhaps one should point out that it was not the case that economic reforms surfaced suddenly in 1991. There were some reforms in the 1980s also, although that cycle of reforms was certainly not as comprehensive as the reforms attempted since 1991. However, it was tempting to correlate the reforms of the 1980s with the increase in growth and argue that with more systematic and comprehensive reforms, even higher rates of growth should be possible. So we had the reforms of the 1990s and during the Eighth Plan (1992-97), the annual average GDP growth went up to 6.8 per cent. From 3.5 per cent to 5.5 per cent was a jump. So was the jump from 5.5 per cent to 6.8 per cent. Growth has slowed down since 1997. But that is a point we will return to later.

6.8 per cent is an average for the period 1992 to 1997. Perhaps more significant is what happened between 1994-95 and

1996-97. For two of those years (1994-95 and 1995-96), growth crossed seven per cent. And in one year (1996-97), it crossed eight per cent. Eight per cent is therefore possible and eight per cent is also the targeted GDP growth in the Tenth Plan (2002-07). Because the rate of population growth has begun to slow, the 6.8 per cent growth in national income becomes a 4.6 per cent increase in per capita income. This has never happened in India since Independence. At the moment, the rate of population growth is around 1.8 per cent or 1.9 per cent. In the next ten years, it should slow down to around 1.5 per cent. If the Indian economy grows in the next ten years at eight per cent, that will mean an increase in per capita income by 6.5 per cent. With an enormous increase in income and consumption.

Economic Growth

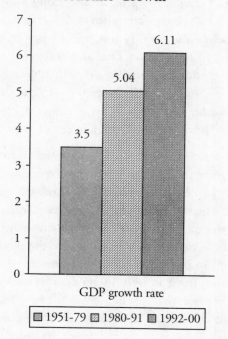

Source: India Development Report, 2002

Eight per cent isn't impossible. Other countries have done it. Not for a couple of years, but over decades. Take the period from 1975 to 1995, a long enough time period. During this period, Cyprus, Hong Kong, South Korea and China have all grown by more than eight per cent. Thailand has grown by almost eight per cent. And Malaysia and Indonesia have grown by almost seven per cent. Why shouldn't it be possible in India also?

What we need to do to get eight per cent rate of growth is an issue we will come to later. For the moment, let us talk about the link between growth and poverty alleviation. Whenever there has been growth, poverty has dropped. You don't have to wait for hundreds of years or generations. It can be done in 20 or 30 years. Consider the countries I have just mentioned. Poverty, meaning the percentage of population below the national poverty line, is insignificant in Cyprus, Hong Kong and South Korea. Before the East Asian currency crisis, the percentage of population below the poverty line was 15 per cent in Indonesia and Malaysia, 13 per cent in Thailand and 6 per cent in China. Within a generation of between 20 and 30 years, it is possible for poverty to drop from 30 per cent to 15 per cent and below. Provided growth takes place. This message is clear from other countries that have exhibited high rates of growth.

There is a technical reason for these sharp drops in poverty. If you plot income distributions, they typically tend to be log normal. That is, a lot of people have low incomes and few people have high incomes. The income distribution leans to the left, so to speak, if you plot a diagram. When income increases and that thick part of the distribution passes above the poverty line, there are large drops in poverty. That's the reason there are sharp drops in poverty ratios from around 30 per cent to around 15 per cent. Of course, beyond that 15 per cent, further drops in poverty become more difficult to accomplish. It is possible to argue that this is precisely what is likely to happen in India in the next ten years. Provided the growth takes place.

The expression trickle-down is a much-maligned expression. What happens to poverty does indeed depend on the composition of growth, as well as the growth itself. The evidence from other countries does show that trickle down does happen and benefits of growth do percolate down to poorer sections of society. But there must be something to trickle down. What will trickle down if there is no growth?

It's not that trickle down has only occurred in other countries. Consider the experience of different Indian States and their records in terms of increases in State domestic product (SDP). I have already told you that large samples of the NSS (National Sample Survey) are collected infrequently, roughly once every five years. We had such a large sample in 1993-94 and another one in 1999-2000. There is some debate about comparability of 1993-94 data with 1999-2000 data, but that is not relevant for present purposes. We will come back to that point later.

The poor States in India are known as the BIMARU (Bihar, Madhya Pradesh, Rajasthan and Uttar Pradesh) States, with a pun on the word BIMAR. Bihar, MP and UP of course mean their undivided versions. If you look at the poverty ratios in 1993-94, you find this identification of BIMARU with poor is somewhat simplistic. Rajasthan had a poverty ratio of 27.41 per cent and was not quite as bad as the other BIMARU States. On the other hand, Assam and Orissa are not normally included in BIMARU, but are fairly poor. If you consider 1999-2000, you will find the poverty ratio in Rajasthan dropped to 15.28 per cent. The drop was from 22.19 per cent to 15.77 per cent in Andhra. In 1999-2000, the poor States continued to be Bihar, MP, UP, Assam and Orissa. Undivided Bihar and Orissa were the only States with poverty ratios more than 40 per cent. More interestingly, whenever SDP grew fast, or per capita SDP grew fast, there were sharp drops in poverty ratios. Among major States, this happened in Andhra Pradesh, Gujarat, Karnataka,

Kerala, MP, Maharashtra, Tamil Nadu, Rajasthan and West Bengal. In each of these States, per capita SDP grew by more than 3.5 per cent and poverty ratios dropped sharply. Conversely, in the 1990s, per capita SDP grew by less than 2 per cent in undivided Bihar, UP and Orissa. And in these States, there have been very marginal declines in poverty.

So trickle down not only works across countries. It also works across States. What do we need to do to step up growth is thus the key question.

Increasing Growth

How do we increase growth? Growth is the key. It is a necessary condition to removing poverty. If we don't have growth, any redistributive policies will merely amount to redistributing poverty, not redistributing wealth. To make a dent on poverty, the size of the cake has to increase. This is evident from the experiences of other countries. It is evident from India's experience at an all-India level. It is also clear from the performance of different Indian States.

Any text-book of economics will tell us that there are factors or inputs required for production. Four such factors or inputs are usually talked about – land, labour, capital and entrepreneurship. To increase output and to increase growth, we have to increase inputs in production. Land is of course relevant only for agriculture. Entrepreneurship is the trait of risk-taking and is the input that economists understand the least, although without entrepreneurship, none of the other inputs can work. De facto, economic discussions of increasing output thus boil down to labour and capital. To increase output, increase use of labour and capital. This is known as the extensive way of increasing production. Alternatively, it may not be possible to increase use of labour and capital. In that case, increase the efficiency of their use. This is known as the intensive way of increasing production.

What is capital and how does it increase? Capital is anything that represents productive potential of an economy. Hence, machinery and equipment, buildings and inventory are all capital and any additions to these is known as investment. To boost growth, one has to increase investment. Text-books will also tell us that developing countries like India lack capital. Capital is scarce. Labour is abundant. In a capital scarce country, the trick to growth is to increase investments. That's precisely what we have been trying to do since 1951, when the First Five Year Plan was formulated.

Economists love models. These days, economic models have become complicated. But a simple model continues to be taught to students. This model is known as the Harrod-Domar model and was the basis for the First Five Year Plan (1951-56). Two economists named Harrod and Domar first formulated this model independently. Hence the name. Although, economic models have become more complicated now, the essential contention of the Harrod-Domar model hasn't changed.

India is a capital scarce country. We have to increase investments? How do we increase investments? Investments can be funded through domestic savings or foreign savings. For example, both foreign direct investments and borrowing amount to use of foreign savings to finance domestic investments. But use of foreign savings wasn't an important option for India historically. Before 1991, FDI was virtually precluded. Therefore, the focus was on domestic savings. Since 1950-51, the domestic savings rate (expressed as a share of GDP or gross domestic product) has increased quite a bit. It was 8.9 per cent in 1950-51 and increased to 23.1 per cent in 1990-91. There is talk of increasing it still further, but we will come back to this point later on. Simultaneously, the investment rate (again expressed as a share of GDP) has also increased. It was 8.9 per cent in 1950-51 and increased to 22.9 per cent in 1990-91. To get back to Harrod-Domar, the model states the following. GDP growth is the investment rate divided by the capital/output ratio. The capital/output ratio is the amount of units of capital required to produce one unit of output. It is a measure of the productivity of capital. The higher the capital/output ratio, the more inefficiently capital is being used. The lower the capital/output ratio, the more efficiently capital is being used. In the absence of foreign savings, the investment rate is nothing but the domestic savings rate. So the growth rate is the domestic savings rate divided by the capital/output ratio. If the savings rate is 12 per cent and the capital/output ratio is 4, the economy will grow at 3 per cent. If the savings rate is 20 per cent and the capital/output ratio is 4, the economy will grow at 5 per cent. If the savings rate can be increased to 28 per cent and the capital/output ratio is 4, the economy will grow at 7 per cent. Simple.

I have just said that since 1950-51, the domestic savings rate and the investment rate have both increased. Yet, I have also said earlier that till the end of the 1970s, the Indian economy showed low rates of growth. The so-called Hindu rate of growth. What went wrong in the idea of increasing domestic savings and investments and thereby ensuring higher rates of growth? Simple again. In our obsession with increasing investments, we didn't pay adequate attention to the efficiency with which capital was being used. That was the problem.

If the savings rate is 24 per cent and the capital/output ratio is 4, the economy will grow at 6 per cent. But if the capital/output ratio is 3, with the same savings rate of 24 per cent, the economy can grow at 8 per cent. As I said, the capital/output ratio measures the efficiency of capital use. More accurately, we should use the incremental capital/output ratio, also known as ICOR. That measures the productivity of additional capital rather than the entire capital stock. Today, India's ICOR is around 4.2, although at one point it had crossed 6. Other countries have ICORs of around 2.5. Why should our ICOR be so high? By the way, the ICOR during the Ninth Five Year Plan

(1997-2002) was 4.5. The Tenth Five Year Plan (2002-2007) expects real GDP growth of 8 per cent and that is based on the ICOR dropping to 3.6.

All kinds of reasons can be given for our high ICORs. We have chosen large projects instead of small ones and large projects have higher ICORs. Large projects require large doses of capital. ICORs also increase if projects aren't completed on time, because costs are inflated. All this is true. But also ask yourself the following question. What ensures productivity and efficiency? If you look around this world, you will discover that without competition, you don't get efficiency and productivity. Competition is essential. The point about competition is one I will illustrate in the next chapter. For the moment, note that because of lack of competition and monopolies, we had high ICORs. So the promise of higher growth that we got from Harrod-Domar never materialized. Although I have expressed it in terms of Harrod-Domar, that's what the reforms since 1991 are all about. They are about increasing competition and efficiency. Through that route, they are about increasing growth.

4

Competition and Efficiency

IT is impossible to get efficiency without competition.

I have not been to my bank for years. That is a trip that is no longer necessary. Almost everything that you want done can be accomplished through ATMs. So we no longer care whether banks are on strike or not. Even if it is twelve in the night, I can use an ATM to take out money. And the notes I get are crisp and new. I am not exaggerating. On several occasions, the notes have been so crisp that I have cut my fingers. Today, our entire household has moved away from public sector banks. But there was a time, not very long ago, when we had accounts with public sector banks.

When I deposit my money with a bank, who is doing whom a favour? Is the bank doing me a favour by accepting my money? Or am I doing the bank a favour by depositing my money with the bank? I am inclined to think that I am doing the bank a favour. However, every time I went to my public sector bank, I felt as if the bank was doing me a big favour. I used to go to take out money that was rightfully mine. It was money that I had kept in the bank. Yet, every time, I would have to wait like a beggar for one hour. At the end of the wait, I would get a bundle of fifty rupee notes stapled thirteen times with seven rubber bands. And when I broke open the staples, I would discover that half the notes were useless. I am not for the moment concerned about the broader issues of gains and losses from bank nationalization. Yes, public sector banks may have social responsibilities. Yes, they may have to open branches in remote and rural areas. Yes, they may not have been able to pay much attention to profitability. But what has that got to do with the treatment I receive as a customer? My bank branch was supposed to open at 9.30 in the morning. The clerk was never there till 10.00. We had to wait. We had to wait because he was having tea and chatting to other clerks. We didn't have to wait because he had to reach this branch from a remote village.

Have you ever tried to claim insurance after your car has been stolen? If you have paid the premium, the money is yours by right, isn't it? Assuming of course that you have been honest about your car being stolen. Have you ever tried to claim life insurance? Since 1986, we have had the Consumer Protection Act (COPRA). If you track cases filed by consumers under COPRA, you will discover how difficult it is to claim insurance, of the life or non-life variety.

We forget very easily. But it wasn't very long ago when we had to bribe to get gas or telephone connections. MPs had discretionary quotas for granting gas and telephone connections on priority basis. So you had to hunt out a MP. I don't remember, but I have been told that in the 1970s, MPs also had discretionary quotas for HMT watches. Have you forgotten the kind of treatment you used to get with Indian Airlines? I remember an incident from 1992. There is a gentleman who used to work for a trading concern in Indonesia. Every year, he would come to India to select students from management institutes. In December 1992, Indian Airlines was on strike and this gentleman had come to India to recruit students from Delhi and Mumbai. Having interviewed students in Delhi, he wanted to go to Mumbai. And the only way that was possible was for him to fly

Delhi-Bangkok and do Bangkok-Mumbai again. He told me that he would never come back to India. I can't blame him. Of course, the last 11 years have changed many things.

I am not deliberately trying to pick on the public sector. Ownership is irrelevant. Lack of competition fosters inefficiency even in the private sector. Maruti made its appearance in India in the mid-1980s. Before that, all of us were driving around in four-wheeled contraptions that would not be recognized as cars anywhere else in the world. A mere change of the bumper led to a change in a model for the Ambassador. It was said of the Ambassador that every part of the car made a noise except the horn. In 1995, we decided to book for a Fiat Uno. We never went through with the booking eventually, but we thought about it. At that time, a Fiat Uno was parked on display at a shopping centre in Delhi and we went to see what this new car looked like. The only part of the car we bothered about was the rear windows. Do you know why? At one time, we used to possess a Fiat. The old kind, 1100 – not NE-118 or Uno or Palio. And we always had a problem with this car. The rear windows would fall down. The car would go to the garage. The mechanic would fix the windows and within a week, they would fall down again. Before competition, came in, every Fiat produced in India since the 1950s has had such a problem.

Maruti brought a revolution to the automobile sector. How long has the Maruti 800 been around? Since the mid-1980s. That's more than 19 years. For more than 19 years we have known that all it takes to open the lock of a Maruti 800 is a scale inserted under the lining. Does Maruti not know about this? Is Maruti in league with car thieves? Is there a big technological issue? Will costs go up significantly? Of course not. Maruti saw no reason to change the lock because there was no competition in the 800 segment. It is only after competition came in that locks began to improve in this segment.

The issue is not public sector or private sector. Regardless of the sector, efficiency doesn't improve without competition. A monopolist sees no reason to change. Even if the monopolist doesn't change anything, huge profits will still be made. In the absence of competition, the market is protected and profitable. No need to upgrade technology, reduce costs, improve efficiency or offer consumers a better deal. Lack of competition is a major distinction between economic policies followed in India and in South-East India. It is lack of competition that has driven down growth. And it is competition that needs to be pushed through the reforms.

The Lack of Competition

As already argued, competition is necessary for efficiency and efficiency is necessary for growth. Lack of competition is also bad for the consumer. Why was there limited competition before 1991? What policies restricted competition? There is a fairly long list. But the main culprits were eight specific policies.

(1) Imports can bring in competition. But there were all kinds of restrictions on free imports. There were quantitative restrictions (QRs) on free imports and an import licensing regime. That apart, there were very high import duties on imports. The highest import duty was more than 350 per cent. Not on personal baggage, on other items as well. Hence competition through imports was ruled out.

(2) In exactly the same way, competition through foreign direct investment (FDI) was ruled out. Before 1991, FDI wasn't welcome. It was excluded in many sectors, such as consumer goods. And when it was allowed, there were all kinds of restrictions on the maximum foreign equity permitted. From the point of view of the consumer, one should remember that the more the competition, the better it is. The colour of the

competition, national or foreign, doesn't matter. The argument that consumers should be exploited on nationalistic grounds is nonsense.

(3) Domestic manufacturing was subjected to industrial licensing and such licences weren't freely available to all those who wanted them. Those favoured by the government obtained such licences and one had to spend considerable resources to be thus favoured by the government. There were long queues in government offices in Delhi to obtain licences and companies had to set up offices in Delhi just for the sake of obtaining these licences. With limited licences and resultant shortages, the market became one of monopolies or oligopolies. Not only did this mean high profits, it also meant consumers could be freely exploited. We have forgotten shortages of gas connections or telephone connections now. We also tend to think that licensing is over after the post-1991 reforms. That's only partly true, meaning it is true of industry. For agriculture and many services sectors, licensing still remains and we will return to this point later.

(4) There was also a law known as the Monopolies and Restrictive Trade Practices (MRTP) Act, enacted in 1970. In the 1960s, two government committees (the Dutt and Hazari committees) were set up. These arrived at the stupendous conclusion that monopolistic conditions were developing in Indian industry. Of course, and it didn't need government committees to determine what was obvious to everyone. Licensing leads to monopolies. The answer to elimination of monopolies was therefore an end to licensing. Instead of this common sense approach, those two government committees led to the MRTP Act. We will probably come back to the MRTP Act later. For the moment,

note that thanks to the MRTP Act, certain companies came to be classified as MRTP companies. And such companies were subjected to a fresh round of licensing, in addition to the usual industrial licensing. That is, MRTP companies needed additional licences to set up new plants or expand capacity in existing plants.

(5) Other than the MRTP Act, there was the Foreign Exchange Regulation Act (FERA). FERA was originally passed during World War II, under the Defence of India Rules of 1939. At that time, FERA was meant to be a temporary provision to handle war-time shortages. But after Independence, FERA became permanent. Instead of removing foreign exchange shortages, planning made foreign exchange shortages permanent. Indeed, foreign exchange shortages became more acute over time. So the 1947 version of FERA was replaced with a stricter 1973 version of FERA. We will discuss FERA later. For the moment, under FERA, some companies came to be classified as FERA companies and these had further conditions imposed on them. Competition was restricted even further.

(6) Some sectors were reserved for production by the public sector. This was not just for manufacturing, but also for public utilities. Since private sector entry was prohibited, even when it was possible, competition was curtailed.

(7) Reservations existed not only for the public sector, but also for small-scale industries (SSI). Such reservations increased in importance in the second half of the 1960s and the 1970s. When an item was selected for reservation in the SSI sector, there were large units that were also producing that item. Were these asked to close down? No, their production was frozen at the prevailing level. There are not too many instances of

small firms offering successful competition to large firms. Competition to these existing large firms would have come through further entry of new large firms. But that was precluded because of SSI reservation. That is the reason SSI reservations worked against competition.

(8) Government procurement policy also worked against competition. There were purchase and price preferences in favour of domestic production, the public sector and the SSI sector.

Other policies can be added. But these eight are the core ones that restricted competition. Notice that policies restricting competition became more accentuated in the late 1960s and early 1970s.

It is not the case that protection only harmed consumers. Protection also harmed producers. It wasn't just finished consumer goods that were subjected to high protection. Protection also characterized raw materials and intermediate products, used as inputs in production. These resulted in high costs and inferior quality of inputs, adversely affecting domestic production. India became a high cost economy. Lack of competition meant that Indian industry had no incentive to upgrade technology, reduce costs or improve efficiency. Even if these things weren't done, huge profits could be made in the protected and profitable domestic market.

It is extremely unfortunate that the unintended consequences of these policies weren't foreseen at the time. First, the protection granted was to industry and this artificially distorted incentives away from agriculture and towards industry. Remember that two-thirds of the Indian population is employed in agriculture. Remember also that agricultural income may not be taxed. But distorting terms of trade against agriculture is also a form of taxation.

Second, the protection system was completely arbitrary. It had no logic. For several years, our country has had an exim (export import) policy. Before QRs were discarded, the most important element in exim policy was QRs, especially QRs on imports. Before 1991, you would find a schedule in exim policy that told you which items could be exported after obtaining a licence. In that category, you would find an item that said "cattle and other animals". And just below that, there was another category that said "donkeys". Doesn't this suggest to you that some Joint Secretary in Commerce Ministry has seriously scrutinized the issue and decided that donkeys can't be clubbed with other animals, but deserve to be in a special category of their own?

5

Unintended Consequences and the 1990-91 Crisis

BAD policies have unintended consequences and I gave some examples in the last pages. The protection was completely arbitrary. Let me give you the example of Pomfret fishes. You could export Pomfrets. But there was a condition. If the Pomfret was caught in the waters of 10 different ports, which were named, the fish could be exported if it weighed more than 300 grammes. If it was caught anywhere else, it could be exported if it weighed more than 200 grammes. Imagine what this did to you as an exporter of Pomfrets. Customs would have to weigh each fish and then try to figure out whether it had been caught in the waters of those 10 ports or somewhere else. *Beche-de-mer* is a kind of sea cucumber. That could be exported if it was longer than three inches. You had similar arbitrary instances for imports also.

The simple point is that licensing and protection was arbitrary and without economic rationale. Industrialists lobbied to obtain licences and protection for themselves and prevent it for others. This led to a lot of time and resources being frittered away in useless activities that economists call directly unproductive economic activities. Some of it was of course bribes.

The policy also led to an anti-export bias. The domestic market was protected and profitable. One could survive there and make huge profits without upgrading technology, improving efficiency and reducing costs. But the export market was competitive. One had no hope of surviving there. Therefore, Indian industry had no desire to export. Or even if it wanted to export, it couldn't survive in the globally competitive export market. Calculations show that import substitution policies meant that the import substituting or domestic market was 25 per cent more profitable than the export market. This lasted till the mid-1980s. In the second half of the 1980s, the protection to the domestic market dropped a bit. However, the point is why should Indian industry want to export? As a country, we of course wanted those exports, because we needed foreign exchange to pay for imports of crude oil and machinery and equipment.

We wanted uncompetitive Indian industry to export and this was only possible through a complicated system of export incentives. The infant industry argument went on and on and the infants never became adults.

I have already mentioned the shoddy treatment that consumers, domestic or foreign, obtained.

Both supporters and opponents of reforms tend to over-simplify when they argue that 1991 marked a watershed. There was a revolution in the Indian economy. This is an over-simplification, because economic reforms are evolutionary rather than revolutionary. As I have said earlier, there were limited attempts to reform the economy in the mid-1980s and one cannot ignore this element of continuity.

It wasn't the case that the IMF or the World Bank suddenly told us in 1991 what was wrong with the Indian economy. What was wrong with the Indian economy has been known for years. Especially since the 1990s, the problems have been highlighted by a large number of Indian economists, Jagdish Bhagwati being the most prominent. Arguments for reform have been iterated in the reports of a large number of government committees – the Alexander Committee of 1977, the first Tandon Committee of 1980, the second Tandon Committee of 1981 or the Abid Hussain Committee of 1984. My favourite is the Dagli Committee of 1978. If you read the Dagli Committee's report, you will find today's reform agenda stated in its entirety. The jargon may be slightly different, but the content is all there. The point is that the reform agenda is not due to the IMF or the World Bank. If anything, the IMF or the World Bank was only recycling arguments that originated within the country. Let's not unnecessarily blow up the importance of the IMF or the World Bank. Also, quite often people say that there has been no debate about economic reforms in India. That's rubbish. What have all these reports been about then?

The debate had already taken place. But at that time, no policy maker wanted to listen. Because there was no immediate economic crisis.

Reforms were triggered by a balance of payments (BoP) crisis in 1990-91. Without that BoP crisis, there would probably have been no reforms and the Indian economy would have continued to chug along at the Hindu rate of growth of 3.5 per cent.

Those who are familiar with the Indian economy know the reasons for the BoP crisis of 1990-91. The first component in any BoP statement is the trade account or merchandise account. This is exports minus imports. Since 1949-50, India has had balance of trade surpluses in only two years, 1972-73 and 1976-77. In every other year, there was a balance of trade deficit. The question before a policy maker has therefore been virtually unchanged since 1947. How do you finance that balance of trade deficit?

Beyond the trade account, there are invisibles like banking, insurance, shipping and tourism. These also give rise to foreign exchange receipts and payments. When invisibles are added to the trade account, one gets the current account. Capital account transactions also give rise to foreign exchange receipts and payments. When the capital account is added to the current account, one gets an overall picture of the bop.

To get back to the question of financing the trade deficit, India used two routes. First, it used capital inflows through borrowing. FDI and foreign institutional investments are also capital inflows. But before 1991, these were precluded. So India resorted to borrowing. Borrowing can be from three different sources – bilateral (other governments), multilateral or the commercial market. Increasingly, bilateral and multilateral sources of borrowing became difficult for India to obtain. Increasingly, in the 1980s, a large chunk of India's borrowing was from the commercial market. These are hard loans, with higher rates of interest and shorter timeframes for repayment than the soft loans of the bilateral or multilateral variety. A large chunk of India's borrowing was for 180 days. At the end of 180 days, one borrowed again and rolled the credit over and over again. Whether one can do this successfully or not depends on how much faith the international commercial banking system has in India as a credit worthy country. And in 1990-91, primarily because of political uncertainties, two major international credit rating agencies rapidly downgraded India's credit rating.

In addition, through the invisibles route, India had used remittances from Indian workers settled abroad (often in the Middle East) to finance the trade deficit. With the Gulf War, this disappeared. Petroleum prices shot up. Conventional exports to the Middle East suffered. There were repatriation costs to bring back Indians who were stranded there. NRIs withdrew their deposits from India. What more does one need for a crisis?

6

Handling the 1990-91
Crisis and QRs

I have already described the 1990-91 balance of payments (BoP) crisis. In January 1991, foreign exchange reserves were 1 billion US dollars. India came close to defaulting on external debt obligations. You must also remember that India has an impeccable record in repaying debt on time. India has never asked for rescheduling or postponements. Therefore, it was also psychologically important that there was no actual default in 1991. At the time we are talking about, there was no government in power. The only organization that could take some decision or the other was the RBI. The RBI pledged gold in London and raised foreign exchange against that, so that we didn't actually default. Subsequently, that gold has been redeemed.

Sometimes, people argue that there was no alternative to reforms in 1991. This is the TINA (there is no alternative) argument. That's not quite true. There was an alternative, but that wouldn't have been a desirable one from the point of view of the economy. We could have clamped down on imports. Tightened up quantitative restrictions and raised import duties. But that would also have shackled economic growth. Hence, this wasn't an attractive option. I have already outlined the reasons why we should have reformed. Before 1991. The clever option therefore was to use the pretext of the 1990-91 BoP crisis to engineer reforms. And that was indeed what was done. The reforms can be divided into an external sector component and a domestic component, although the two impinge on one another. First, let us talk about the external sector reforms.

External sector reforms belong to five strands – elimination of quantitative restrictions (QRs), changes in export subsidies, reductions in import duties, liberalization in foreign investment regimes and changes in exchange control and exchange rates. Let's take these one by one. Remember that all reforms didn't happen suddenly in 1991. But they did happen step by step. Before talking about these reforms, it is also necessary to get another proposition clear, because this often causes unnecessary confusion. Protection is always bad for any economy. Protection obviously benefits inefficient producers. But such protection is not costless, since costs have to be borne by consumers. These consumers need not always be consumers of final consumer goods. They can also be producers themselves. That is, they can be consumers of raw materials and intermediate goods. Economic theory can be used to prove that the benefits from protection (which accrue to producers) are lower than the costs of protection (which are borne by consumers). That is, in net welfare terms, the economy loses and there is a deadweight loss as a result of protection.

Having said this, the first item is elimination of QRs, on both imports and exports. Before 1991, India's imports (and exports) belonged to one of four categories. There were prohibited or banned products which could not be imported (or exported). Second, there were canalized items that could only be traded through designated state trading enterprises like STC or MMTC. Third, there were items that required a specific import or export licence. Fourth, there were items that were on open general licence (OGL). Actually, the name OGL is a bit of a misnomer. Because OGL meant you didn't actually need a licence. Imports (or exports) were open. However, you did have to pay required import duties. Once reforms started, at least for imports, a fifth category was started. This was known as the special import licence (SIL) category. SILs were granted to specific categories of exporters and these could be used to import a subset of items on the restricted list. Thanks to reforms and partly due to a phenomenon I will mention in a moment, all QRs have now gone. Usually, the 8-digit harmonized classification system is followed in classifying exports and imports. Under this, around 10,500 items are described. Before 1991, 8000 imports out of these 10,500 used to be on QRs. Today, the figure is slightly over 500. Everything is on OGL. That shows how much reforms have proceeded.

On QRs, a point that is not always obvious to non-economists needs to be mentioned. All protection is bad. But if there has to be protection, that is better done through import duties than through QRs. In the case of import duties, at least customs revenue accrues to the government. But in the case of QRs, beneficiaries are those who obtain these scarce import licenses and can reap a premium by selling them. Resources are also wasted in lobbying to obtain these scarce licenses. Economists call these directly unproductive economic (DUPE) activities. Hence, import duties are preferable. Since QRs are inefficient, India's unilateral reforms also sought to reduce QRs and by April 1997, the number of import items on the QR list dropped from 8000 to 2700. The WTO (World Trade Organization) is blamed for all kinds of things under the sun. There is an impression floating around that these remaining 2700 QRs also had to be phased out because of the WTO. But this impression is not quite true.

WTO was set up in January 1995. Its precursor is GATT (General Agreement on Tariffs and Trade), set up in 1947 with 23 countries as founder members. India happens to be one of these founder members. So India has been bound by these GATT rules since 1947. GATT also recognizes that QRs are inefficient. Therefore, Article XI of GATT says that if imports are to be restricted, that should be done through tariffs and not QRs. That is, QRs are illegal under GATT. Much before the WTO. The fact that we continued to have QRs was because of another GATT article known as Article XVIIIB. This said the following. QRs were illegal under Article XI. But if a country had balance of payment (BoP) problems, under Article XVIIIB, it would be freed from the general prohibition on QRs. India thus justified continued use of QRs by invoking Article XVIIIB. By arguing that the BoP was in bad shape.

We can argue about what success the reforms have had in changing the Indian economy. But there is one area where no arguments are possible. Clearly and unambiguously, there have been improvements in the external sector. It is impossible to argue that the BoP is in bad shape. It is impossible to argue that we continue to need Article XVIIIB. On this, we lost a dispute before WTO. The WTO ruled that we can no longer use Article XVIIIB. That's the reason QRs were phased out from April 2001. Strictly speaking, not all QRs have been phased out. QRs are also permitted under Articles XX and XXI of GATT, on grounds of protecting the environment, security and things like that. Those QRs still remain. These are the 500 items that are still on QRs.

7

Tariffs

WE have been discussing external sector reforms. I talked about quantitative restrictions (QRs). However, imports are restricted not only through QRs, but also through high tariffs.

But before talking about tariffs, we need to digress a bit on the WTO (World Trade Organization). The WTO has agreements on various subjects and this includes tariffs. As a member and signatory to the WTO and consequent agreements, India has to adhere to WTO commitments. There are two kinds of commitments that any member country has before the WTO. The first is called a reduction commitment. When a country has a reduction commitment of a certain percentage, that means it has agreed to reduce tariffs by that percentage. The base on which reductions have to be made and the time frame over which reductions are to be made, are also part of the commitment. In addition, there is something called a binding commitment, with bound rates. Bound rates set a maximum or cap to tariffs. So if a country has a binding commitment at a certain percentage, tariffs cannot be set higher than this level. The reduction and binding commitments operate simultaneously. Both types of commitments have to be adhered to. The present commitments India has, follow from the Uruguay Round (1986-94) negotiations. As most people know, further negotiations are going on at WTO. When those commitments surface, there will be additional bindings and reductions. But today, we have the Uruguay Round commitments.

The tariff commitments again vary, depending on whether we are talking about industrial or manufactured products or agricultural products. First, let us talk about industrial products. At the Uruguay Round, India made a reduction commitment tariff line by tariff line. That is, the commitment is at the level of individual items. However, this works out to an average reduction of 30 per cent. On the 1990 base. Tariffs haven't declined only because of the WTO. They have also been slashed thanks to unilateral reforms, because of the recognition that protection leads to inefficiencies and welfare losses. Because of these unilateral tariff reductions, the Uruguay Round's reduction commitments are now irrelevant. India has already reduced tariffs by more than the Uruguay Round requires. That leaves the binding commitment, or the maximum. This is either 25 per cent or 40 per cent. This means that we look at actual tariffs in the year 1990. If in the year 1990, actual tariffs were over 40 per cent, India has agreed to bind them at 40 per cent. No higher. And if in the year 1990, actual tariffs were less than 40 per cent, India has agreed to bind them at 25 per cent. No higher. There are some sectors that are presently excluded from India's binding and reduction commitments. Examples are consumer goods, fertilizers, non-ferrous metals and petroleum products. Obviously, if there are further commitments thanks to future WTO negotiations, this will change.

This leaves agricultural products. The reduction commitments are again irrelevant. Generally, for agricultural products, India's bound rate is 100 per cent for primary products, 150 per cent for processed products and 300 per cent for some varieties of edible oils. There are some instances where bindings are at 40 per cent, 50 per cent, 60 per cent or 70 per cent. On an average, India's agricultural bound rate is 117 per cent. Except edible oils, and perhaps dairy, most Indian agro products are price competitive by global standards. Therefore, there should be no great fear of a deluge of imports, even if duties were lower. As things stand, tariffs permitted are fairly high. There were a few agricultural commodities where India had 0 per cent bindings because of historical reasons. Nothing to do with the Uruguay Round, but going back much before that. This was because of the belief that QRs would continue. If you want to deviate from GATT or WTO commitments, that can be done by renegotiating agreements and compensating trading partners for the resultant losses. This has now been done for the 0 per cent bindings.

Reduction in Tariff Rates

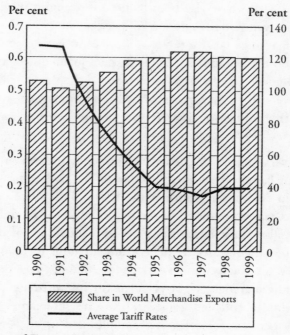

Source: Ministry of Finance, Economic Survey

Tariffs of course have many components. First, there is a basic customs duty. Second, there is a countervailing duty, equal to domestic excise and levied so that domestic manufacturers aren't at a disadvantage. Countervailing duty is also levied against unwarranted export subsidies used by other countries. Third, there is a special additional duty (SAD), equal to domestic sales tax. Fourth, there may be surcharges, which have now gone. Fifth, there may be anti-dumping duties or safeguard duties. Anti-dumping duties are levied against unfair competition from abroad. Safeguard duties (or safeguard QRs) can be imposed as temporary aberration from WTO commitments if a country is threatened with a sudden import surge. India's WTO commitments (reduction and binding) are on the basic customs duty. Not on the other parts.

That's about the WTO. As I said earlier, because of unilateral reforms, tariffs have also been reduced. Economic Survey tells us that the average tariff rate was 47 per cent in 1990-91. In 2001-02, the average tariff rate was 16 per cent, with especially high tariffs on food products, chemicals, man-made fibres, metals and capital goods. Tariffs have been reduced thanks to reforms. But they are still fairly high, especially in comparison with other countries and this comparison includes other developing countries.

Several committees have recommended further reductions and this has also been mentioned in several budget speeches. The latest in committee reports is the Kelkar Task Force's report on indirect taxes, submitted to the government in December 2002. The Kelkar Task Force has a recommended set of duties for 2004-05 and another set of recommendations for 2006-07. Let me give you the recommendations for 2006-07. Five per cent for basic raw materials, eight per cent for intermediate goods, ten per cent for finished goods that are not consumer durables, twenty per cent for consumer durables and up to 150 per cent for agricultural goods and demerit goods. There are separate suggestions for automobiles, cellular phones and petroleum products. Most economists will argue for a common rate. How do I know what is a raw material, what is an intermediate, what is a finished good and what is a consumer durable? Why should I distinguish between industry and agriculture? Most non-economists will disagree.

But everyone will agree that thanks to reforms, tariffs have been slashed and this is desirable.

8

Export Subsidies

HAVING talked about QRs (quantitative restrictions) and tariffs, one should move on to the next major strand of external sector reforms – export subsidies. One should of course distinguish between export subsidies and export incentives. This is a distinction that is important for the WTO as well. An export subsidy occurs when there is some special preferential treatment for exports, as compared to treatment granted to the same product when sold in the domestic market. For example, a lower rate of interest on export credit than on domestic credit is an export subsidy. An income tax exemption on export profits is an export subsidy. An export incentive has no such differentiation. For instance, imported products may be used in producing an item that is eventually exported and there may be import duties paid on the imported products. If these import duties, or domestic indirect taxes, are reimbursed when a product is exported, that's an example of an export incentive. In general, export subsidies are prohibited by WTO. Export incentives are allowed. I will come back to this point in a moment.

Before 1991, we had all kinds of export subsidies. Thanks to protection, Indian industry was uncompetitive. It wouldn't have been able to survive in the competitive international market. But we needed exports and foreign exchange to pay for say crude oil imports. To persuade uncompetitive Indian industry to export, export subsidies were introduced and there were several of these, the most prominent being the cash compensatory support (CCS) scheme. Each product had a CCS rate, according to which, cash was disbursed to exporters. And this rate varied from product to product. How could one possibly know what CCS rate an export item deserved? The answer is that the system was completely arbitrary and encouraged lobbying to ensure a higher CCS rate for one's exported product. Thanks to the unilateral process of reforms, export subsidies have now been largely unified across sectors. They don't vary from product to product or sector to sector.

There is one additional point. Before 1991, the rupee was over-valued and the exchange rate was unrealistic. This made Indian exporters artificially uncompetitive. Now that the exchange rate has become realistic and market-determined, the need for artificial export subsidies has also disappeared.

I said that export subsidies are prohibited by the WTO. Let me be a bit more careful. There are two kinds of subsidy agreements in the WTO, one for industrial or manufactured products and this is governed by the subsidies and countervailing measures (SCM) agreement. In addition, agricultural products have special treatment and that is governed by the agreement on agriculture (AOA). For industrial products, the SCM divides export subsidies into three categories – red, amber and green. Hence, this is known as the traffic light principle. Red export subsidies are prohibited by the WTO and the trading partner can take action if such prohibited export subsidies are used. Action means levying countervailing duties against such subsidized exports. Amber export subsidies are permitted by the WTO. But if such export subsidies are used, the trading partner can still take action. Green export subsidies are permitted by the WTO and trading partners are not allowed to take action against these.

Section 80 HHC or their variants and a lower rate of interest on export credit are instances of red export subsidies. They are prohibited. However, there is a catch. A country that has a per capita income of less than 1000 US dollars is freed from this prohibition. Because India's per capita income is lower than 1000 US dollars, the prohibition on red export subsidies doesn't therefore apply to India. If subsidies like Section 80 HHC are progressively being phased out, that's because of unilateral and internal reform compulsions. Not because of something the WTO requires. There is a further caveat to this 1000 US dollars kind of clause. If in any particular product, a country is globally competitive on the world market, for that particular product, you can't have red export subsidies even if your per capita income is less than 1000 US dollars. Globally competitive is interpreted as accounting for more than a 2.5 per cent share of the world market for that product. For example, India is globally competitive in diamonds and jewellery and we can't have red export subsidies for this category. The deadline for elimination was January 2003.

The green export subsidies are what we call export incentives in India. These are allowed by WTO. There are two models for export incentives, to take import duties as an example. I don't pay the import duties to start off with. This is the advance licence kind of model. Second, I may pay the import duties (or domestic indirect taxes) and later get reimbursed. If you like, this is the duty drawback or DEPB (duty exemption passbook) scheme kind of model. The problem with the latter is that duties that are refunded must be exact. That is, I have to establish that those items on which I am refunding duties are actually consumed in the production process. The reimbursement or refund cannot be "excessive". If the refund is excessive, that becomes an amber export subsidy and the trading partner can take action. This is the problem we have with EU (European Union) on DEPB. But, in principle, the same problem can also plague duty drawback. Stated differently, some export subsidies are compatible with WTO and the challenge for Commerce Ministry is to work out a WTO-compatible system of export subsidies. This is what Commerce Ministry has been talking about for some time. Unfortunately, this exercise keeps getting postponed because VAT (value added tax) implementation is postponed. However, there is more to this issue than VAT alone. Most Indian exporters don't have proper books of accounts, separately differentiating domestic sales from export sales. Even if they do, they are reluctant to show these books, especially because there are often two sets of books to avoid paying direct and indirect taxes. Until this problem is solved, regardless of VAT, we will continue to have problems with our trading partners about our export incentive regime.

Finally, you will have read that developed countries like USA, EU, Japan or South Korea have high export subsidies on exports of agricultural products and that distorts world markets. Absolutely true. Agriculture was first liberalized in the course of the Uruguay Round (1986-94) and the liberalization is incomplete and imperfect. Developed countries were supposed to reduce budgetary payments on agro export subsidies by 36 per cent and the volume of subsidized agro exports by 24 per cent. There are lower stipulations for developing countries, but we have no export subsidies specific to agriculture, as opposed to general export subsidies. There are many reasons why developed countries have been able to circumvent this reduction commitment, the most important being that the initial base of export subsidies (on which reductions are to take place) was set artificially high.

9

Foreign Direct Investments

SINCE we are talking about external sector reforms, it is now time to move on to foreign direct investments (FDI).

For any developing country, it is likely that there will be a deficit on the trade account. Exports are never that high. Imports are essential items, such as crude for India. India is no exception to this general principle of having to finance a deficit on the trade account. Since 1947, this has been the most important balance of payments (BoP) management problem. Except for two marginal years in the 1970s (1972-73 and 1976-77), in every other year we have had a trade deficit. How do we finance this trade deficit? That's the policy problem. True, the current account is over and above the trade account. And if we have sufficient net inflows of invisible receipts, the trade deficit may be wiped out and we may even have a current account surplus. That's what has happened to India now, in 2002-03. But in general, until very recently, India has always had a current account deficit. So to state the question differently, how do we finance the current account deficit? Certainly, foreign exchange reserves can temporarily be used to finance the current account deficit. But sooner or later, foreign exchange reserves will run out and that therefore, remains a temporary option. How do we finance the current account deficit permanently?

Share in FDI into Developing Countries

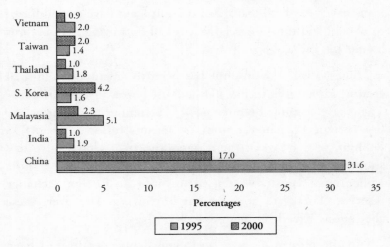

FDI in Some Asian Countries

Capital inflows are the only option and capital inflows can be of two types – borrowing or non-debt creating capital inflows like FDI. Before 1991, there was an emphasis on borrowing and FDI inflows were restricted. There were sectors that FDI couldn't come into. There were equity caps and so on. Both borrowing and FDI have their costs. Costs of borrowing are what have to be paid as interest payments. Costs of FDI are what have to be paid as repatriation of profits and dividends. However, note that the costs of FDI only have to be paid when the venture is successful and actually makes profits. Not otherwise. The costs of borrowing have to be met regardless of the use that is being made of the borrowed funds. Note also that borrowing can be from different sources. Some borrowing can be multilateral (World Bank, IMF, ADB) or bilateral (from individual governments). These are soft loans in the sense that rates of interest are lower and the time frame for repaying loans is longer. Other borrowing can be on the commercial market at commercial terms. These are hard loans, with higher rates of interest and shorter terms for repayment. Most of India's recent loans have been hard loans, because soft loans have been difficult to obtain, and thus, the relative costs of borrowing have become higher for India.

Since 1991, the attempt has been to encourage non-debt creating capital inflows like FDI and use borrowing relatively less. There have certainly been temporary aberrations to this principle. For instance, when economic sanctions followed the 1998 Pokhran tests or when there was a threat of global oil prices shooting up, schemes like Resurgent India Bonds or India Millenium Deposits were used to build up foreign exchange reserves. These are nothing but borrowing. However, these aberrations have been temporary.

In the reform decade, borrowing has generally not been encouraged. In 1991, India's total external debt was 83.8 billion US dollars. In 2002, India's total external debt was 102.0 billion US dollars. The debt has increased, but the rate of increase has slowed down. Also, when talking about an increase, you must remember the following. India's total external debt is in 23 different currencies. To get an overall figure of debt, these have to be converted into a common unit of comparison, called a numeraire. This common unit is usually the US dollar. So whenever the US dollar depreciates against the 22 other currencies, as it has indeed been doing, the total value of external debt expressed in US dollars will go up. Much of the increase in external debt has actually been due to this exchange rate effect. Each year, Finance Ministry now brings out a White Paper on external debt. You will find the details there, not in Economic Survey.

More important than the size of external debt, is the question of whether the country can service this debt and various indicators are used to judge this. For instance, the debt to GDP (gross domestic product) ratio is an indicator. This is around 21 per cent now, nothing much to worry about. If the debt to GDP ratio crosses 25 per cent, we should begin to worry. The ratio of short-term debt to total external debt is another indicator. Short-term debt is defined as debt that is of less than one year's duration and is understandably, volatile. This ratio of short-term debt to total external debt used to be more than 10 per cent before 1991. But is around 3 per cent now. The best indicator of a country's ability to service debt is of course the debt service ratio. This is sometimes expressed as a ratio of export earnings, sometimes as a ratio of current account receipts. It gives us the share of foreign exchange earnings that go towards servicing external debt (principal as well as interest). This ratio was more than 30 per cent in 1991 and is 14 per cent now. So all debt indicators have clearly improved. Ever since 1947, India was a country that depended on foreign aid. One message of the 1990s is an end to foreign aid. India doesn't need foreign aid any more.

To get back to FDI, traditionally two reasons have been given for attracting FDI – known as the two-gap model. We have already talked about the first gap, the foreign exchange gap. FDI helps to tide over the foreign exchange scarcity and is preferable to borrowing. The second gap is known as the savings-investment gap. To understand this, we can go back to the Harrod-Domar model, which I have talked about earlier. In the Harrod-Domar model, the rate of growth of the economy is the investment rate (as a share of GDP) divided by the capital/output ratio. Let's assume India has a savings rate of 24 per cent (as a share of GDP). In the absence of FDI, this will also be the investment rate and if the capital/output ratio is 4, the rate of growth will be 6 per cent. But if FDI comes in, with a domestic savings rate of 24 per cent, the investment rate can perhaps be pushed up to 28 per cent. With the same capital/output ratio of 4, the growth rate now increases to 7 per cent. This is the second gap of the two-gap model.

I personally think some other reasons for attracting FDI are much more important.

I think much more important is the fact that FDI brings competition. Competition is good for consumers. The colour of the competition doesn't matter, nor does its nationality. As a consumer, I refuse to believe that I should be nationalistic and prefer to be exploited by domestic industrialists. I prefer not to be exploited at all and competition (even through FDI) encourages this. New markets are created and this has happened for a whole range of consumer goods, durables as well as fast moving consumer goods.

Because FDI brings competition, it encourages efficiency and also helps upgrade domestic industry and services. Haven't Indian fast food chains improved after foreign fast food chains made their entry? In the Harrod-Domar framework, by stimulating efficiency, FDI reduces the capital/output ratio. Remember also that FDI is preferable to imported foreign goods. In the case of FDI, manufacturing takes place in India and employment generation and other multiplier benefits occur in India. Not in the foreign country. If we are serious about our privatization process, how many Indian companies have that kind of resources? On such a scale? I don't see how we can privatize without FDI. Also, most trade flows are now linked to cross-border investments. An estimated two-thirds of global trade takes place between parent companies and subsidiary companies. How can we hope to push up exports without encouraging FDI? FDI allows access to better technology and marketing channels. Think of food processing. That's a sector characterized by global branding and product differentiation. How can we hope to gate crash into that market without tie-ups with foreign investors?

There will be an argument that foreign companies indulge in unfair and restrictive business practices. Absolutely true. But don't Indian companies do the same? So the argument is against unfair and restrictive business practices, the point is being made that unregulated competition doesn't often work. Absolutely true. Therefore, let us have competition policy instruments to regulate unfair and restrictive business practices. For foreign companies, as well as domestic ones. I don't understand how this becomes an argument specifically against FDI. You will also hear the argument that foreign companies are here to make money, for profits. Of course they are. No one does business for altruistic reasons, not even Indian companies. What is wrong with making profits? What is wrong with even repatriating profits and dividends abroad?

There are some people who argue that FDI should be welcome, but it should come into the sectors we want it to come into. We want FDI for infrastructure, not for consumer goods.

We want it for computer chips, not for potato chips, even though
potato chips have greater employment generation potential. There
are several problems with this argument. First, consumer goods
in India are still protected through high tariffs. So the consumer
goods market is an artificially protected and profitable one. This
distorts resource allocation towards FDI in the consumer goods
sector. Let's reduce tariffs and this distortion will automatically
disappear. Second, we haven't got our infrastructure policies in
place yet. Consider, for example, the problem of appropriate user
charges, which we still haven't resolved. Until we resolve our own
infrastructure policies, how do we expect FDI to come into
infrastructure? This is the reason why a high percentage of FDI
approvals concern infrastructure, but a high percentage of FDI
inflows concern consumer goods. Third, in every country, the
initial flush of FDI inflows is in consumer goods. Returns are
quicker, lower investments are needed. Infrastructure investments
require longer gestation periods and larger sums of money. Until
foreign investors are certain about the policy environment in a
country, FDI doesn't come into infrastructure. Fourth, each
company has a core line of business. Pepsi and Coke sell sugared
water. If we don't allow them to come in, they will simply
disappear to Vietnam. They are not going to build rural schools.

An even more serious argument is the following. Who
decides what is essential and what is not? I don't even know what
is a consumer good. My computer is a consumer good part of
the time, when I play games on it. But it is an input for part
of the time, when I use it for my work. Is some Minister or
Secretary somewhere going to decide what is essential? This is
the case by case approach, which *de facto*, becomes the suitcase
by suitcase approach. Discretion invariably leads to bribery and
corruption.

Let me tell you my favourite story from the early 1990s
about essential and non-essential. A detergent manufacturer was
interested in selling a new variety of detergent and decided to

collect data on sales of washing machines in India. Most people will probably agree that washing machines are elitist. When this detergent manufacturer looked at the figures, it found that 70 per cent of washing machines sold in India were being sold in the Punjab. When it sent a team down to Punjab to find out what was happening, the team found these washing machines were being used for making *lassi*, not for washing clothes. This is the kind of decision the market takes, which no Minister or Secretary can hope to replicate. Are televisions necessities or luxuries? India is a poor country with around 200 million households. Isn't it amazing that 80 million of 200 million households in a poor country possess TV sets? Should we allow FDI in manufacturing television sets? The government is not able to provide clean drinking water. So in remote parts of India now, bottled drinking water is sold. Is that an elitist consumption item?

If you look at our FDI policy today, it is completely open for manufacturing. No restriction on sectors, except of course really identifiable strategic sectors like atomic energy. No equity caps. There is the silly business of no objection certificates from Indian joint venture partners, but we can ignore that for the moment. FDI in services is partly open and partly closed. Meaning that FDI is allowed, but there are sectoral caps, which vary from sector to sector. Remember that globally, most FDI is actually in services. By restricting FDI in services, we are therefore restricting FDI inflows into India. Recently, a committee headed by N.K. Singh recommended throwing open sectoral equity caps in most services sector, primarily because these caps are completely arbitrary. The recommendations have of course not been implemented. And in agriculture and related sectors, FDI is still not allowed.

10

FDI Policy and Numbers

BROADLY speaking, FDI inflows since 1991 belong to two categories – automatic approval and through the Foreign Investment Promotion Board (FIPB). The term automatic approval is itself a misnomer. If everything is automatic, why have the term approval to qualify it? Anyway, the term automatic approval is used for proposals that concern sectors where there are no restrictions or no equity caps or the proposal satisfies the equity cap constraint. This doesn't mean that FDI in other sectors or with higher equity caps won't be considered. But for that, specific approval is needed through FIPB. As more and more liberalization happened, more and more sectors progressively moved from the FIPB channel to the automatic approval channel. I mentioned the recommendations of the N.K. Singh Committee earlier. If these are accepted and implemented, most services sectors will also move to automatic approval. That will only leave a few services and agriculture for FIPB. I would of course like everything to move to automatic approval. We don't need the FIPB. Instead, we can have a Foreign Investment Implementation Authority (FIIA), as the N.K. Singh Committee recommends, to ensure that approvals are actually converted into inflows.

FDI Inflows as Percentage of Approvals

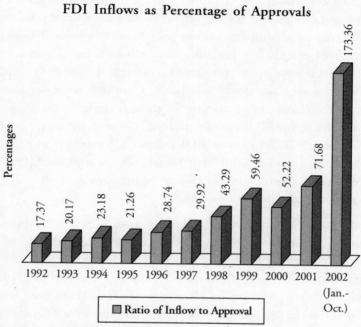

Source: Ministry of Commerce & Industry

Intentions are Increasingly Translated into Action

By the way, we also have unrealistic and unnecessary constraints in manufacturing, despite the liberalization. We have the infamous Press Note 18, introduced by Industry Ministry in December 1998, primarily at the behest of Indian industry. If you are a foreign investor with a technical or financial joint venture (JV) in India, and you want to set up a new subsidiary, Press Note 18 will bite. Because you will need a no objection certificate (NOC) from the Indian joint venture partner if the new subsidiary is in the same or related lines of business. Regardless of whether the old JV is alive or dead. In any sensible country, such decisions will be left to the market and to contractual arrangements (with compensation clauses) between the two original partners. There will be a conflict-of-interest clause and a stipulated cooling-off period (say three years), during which, the new company cannot use the joint venture's brand name (trademark). But India is not a country where we believe in contracts or dispute resolution through the legal system. Hence, the regulator must adjudicate. Common sense suggests that JVs succeed or fail because of commercial considerations. Handholding by FIPB cannot prolong JVs that have outlasted their utility. Globally, most FDI inflows are through mergers, takeovers and acquisitions. Why should India be different? If one is concerned about monopolies that result, competition policy instruments can always be used.

Let's talk about the FDI numbers now. In 1991-92, India obtained 129 million dollars of FDI inflows. Inflows inched up, especially from 1995-96 and touched 3.6 billion in 1997-98. Then came the second round of nuclear tests in Pokhran. Pokhran didn't do anything directly to deter FDI inflows. But economic sanctions and resultant uncertainty did have a deterrent effect. So for three years, from 1998-99 to 2000-2001, inflows ranged between 2 and 2.5 billion. It is only in 2001-02 that inflows inched up to 3.9 billion again. In 2001, China attracted 46.8 billion US dollars worth of FDI. Obviously, we have a very long way to go and the official target of annual FDI inflows worth 10 billion is still far off. Having said this, it is important to make a point. Any economist will readily define investments. However, when it comes to measuring FDI, things are not that simple. For example, do I include reinvested earnings? Do I include investments funded through external commercial borrowings abroad? Answers are not clear in black and white. The IMF has guidelines on what should be included in measuring FDI and there are 12 such forms of FDI. We don't follow this and exclude some of these items. Hence, as compared to IMF guidelines, India under-estimates FDI. And compared to those IMF guidelines, China over-estimates FDI. A government committee has now been appointed to redefine and reclassify India's measurement of FDI. When those recommendations are accepted, India's FDI inflows will move upwards. Some, but not all, of those 12 IMF forms will be included. Compared to today, we will probably discover that we have under-estimated annual FDI inflows by something between 1.5 and 2 billion US dollars. Most FDI inflows into India come through Mauritius. This is because of a special tax avoidance treaty that we have with Mauritius.

Why aren't FDI inflows higher in India? Apart from the measurement problem, it is a fact that the percentage of approvals that gets actually converted into inflows is pretty low. This is known as the conversion ratio and varies between 25 per cent and 30 per cent. Part of the reason is that we haven't got our infrastructure policies in place yet, something I mentioned earlier. More important is the phenomenon of bureaucratic procedures and red tape. After all, when I get a clearance from the FIPB, that is only the first clearance. After that, I have to go to the State and get clearances for land, power, water, labour, environment and so on. That's not easy, not to speak of court interference, thanks to environment-related public interest litigation. The seriousness of these procedural bottlenecks vary from State to State, which is the reason why some States have conversion ratios as high as 50 per cent.

Before leaving FDI, one should mention the WTO. At present, the WTO has only one agreement that governs FDI. This is known as the trade-related investment measures (TRIMs) agreement. Essentially, this prohibits two kinds of policies. First, I cannot have export requirements or dividend balancing requirements. In the process of unilateral reforms, we have already given this up, the last sector for which it existed was consumer goods. Second, I cannot have an indigenisation requirement, known in TRIMs as a local content requirement. Before 1991, we used to have this through the phased manufacturing programme. But this has also been scrapped in the liberalization attempt, although something similar used to exist until fairly recently for automobiles. Therefore, there is nothing in WTO that constrains us today. Of course, there might be further negotiations at WTO on investment and additional commitments that we will then have to abide by. But that is in the future.

11

FERA

AS the final strand of external sector reforms, we are still left with the exchange rate mechanism and the related issue of the Foreign Exchange Regulation Act (FERA).

FERA was originally enacted under the Defence of India Rules of 1939, to handle special exigencies created by World War II. It is remarkable that something originally passed for war-time conditions continued to be on the statute books until fairly recently. Several laws passed during World War II actually remained on the statute books and FERA is one example of this. During the War, foreign exchange was scarce and scarce foreign exchange was needed to pay for food and war equipment. That was the essential idea. The war was over. But scarcity of foreign exchange continued. Therefore, that temporary war-time provision became the FERA statute of 1947. This was still meant to be a temporary provision for 10 years and should have been phased out in 1957. But the advent of planning didn't eliminate the foreign exchange shortage. It merely accentuated it. Thus, in 1957, FERA became a permanent act.

That wasn't all. The foreign exchange shortage became more and more serious. This was due to fallacious policies, which we will talk about later. But these fallacious policies weren't corrected for a long time. Instead, it was thought that there should be more and more controls. And two committees contributed to further tightening up. The first was in 1971 and resulted in a report known as "Leakage of Foreign Exchange through Invoice Manipulation". If the exchange rate is wrong, invoice manipulation is inevitable. But instead of recognizing that the exchange rate was the problem, this report argued for further tightening up. The second report was the 47th report of the Law Commission, submitted in 1972 and titled "Trial and Punishment of Social and Economic Offences". Although not specifically for foreign exchange, this also argued for tightening up. Given these signals, it was perhaps inevitable that the 1947 FERA should be replaced by the 1973 FERA. All this is now of historical interest. But if you compare the 1947 FERA clause by clause with the 1973 FERA, you will discover how much tightening up there was in 1973.

Let me give you three instances to illustrate how silly FERA was. I have not made these up. These are actual FERA cases. First, there was a gentleman named Sharma whose minor son used to collect coins. At that time, the maximum value permitted for a numismatic collection was 10 US dollars. This coin collection was worth more. Because his son was a minor, Mr. Sharma had to pay a fine of Rs. 2000, that too, because the judge was lenient on him. Second, a company exported some goods abroad. Because the goods were not of desired quality, the importer offered to pay 95 per cent of the initially contracted figure and not the entire amount. What was the point of struggling over the remaining 5 per cent, thought the company? We will end up spending much more in litigation. They settled for 95 per cent and this too was held to be a FERA violation. Third, a company exported grapes to the United States. In the process of shipment, the grapes deteriorated a bit and the importer offered to pay only 90 per cent of the contracted amount. The silly Indian exporter agreed and was hauled up for a FERA violation. Do you know what the Indian exporter should have done? He should have brought the grapes back to India and sought RBI permission for re-export at the reduced price.

Finally, thanks to reforms, this outmoded FERA has been scrapped and replaced by the Foreign Exchange Management Act (FEMA).

The idea behind FERA was to control the market for foreign exchange and this also meant the price of foreign exchange. Until the reforms, the exchange rate was also administratively determined by RBI. In principle, there are two types of exchange rate regimes in the world. The first is known as a flexible or floating exchange rate system, where the value of foreign exchange is essentially determined in the market through the forces of demand and supply. Of course, there are gradations and if the Central Bank intervenes quite a bit in the foreign exchange market, that is known as a dirty float. If the Central Bank intervenes only a little, that is known as a clean float. At the other extreme, we have fixed exchange rates, where the exchange rate is administratively determined by the Central Bank. Increasingly, during the 1970s, most countries in the world gave up fixed exchange rates and switched to floating or flexible exchange rates. Not just developed countries, but developing countries also. The fundamental reason behind the switch was quite simple. Private flows increased enormously in importance and it became impossible for Central Banks to precisely estimate demand and supply of foreign exchange. Simultaneously, information technology facilitated such cross-border movements of capital. Any mistake by the Central Bank would therefore throw open the possibility or opportunity for arbitrage. No Central Bank was equipped to deal with this. The market will always out-guess any administrator.

Although there still exists substantive RBI control, this market-determined system is the goal towards which India is gradually progressing.

As I have said, before 1991, the exchange rate of the rupee was administratively decided by RBI. Not only was the exchange rate administratively decided, the rupee was over-valued. By a factor of around 25 per cent. To take an example, let's say the official exchange rate was around 20 rupees to 1 US dollar. (Actually, at the time we are talking about, it was more like 18 rupees to a dollar). In the black market, I would however have had to pay 25 rupees to get 1 US dollar. This is what is meant by over-valuation.

Over-valuation immediately discourages exports. And it is easy to understand why. Suppose I want to quote an item for Rs. 100. With the right exchange rate of 25 rupees to 1 US dollar, I will quote this in the US market for 4 dollars. But with the wrong exchange rate of 20 rupees to 1 US dollar, I will quote it in the US market for 5 dollars and be ousted from the US market by an American producer or an exporter from some other country. Similarly, over-valuation encourages imports artificially. If an import item costs 100 dollars, with the right exchange rate of 25 rupees to 1 US dollar, it will be quoted in India for Rs. 2500. But with the wrong exchange rate of 20 rupees to 1 US dollar, it will be quoted in India for Rs. 2000.

12

Exchange Rate Changes

AS already mentioned, over-valued exchange rates immediately discourage exports and encourage imports. Thus, over-valuation leads to balance of payments problems. To ensure that these balance of payments problems don't become serious, one must have quantitative restrictions on imports or multiple exchange rates, which simply means one exchange rate for exports and another for imports or something like that. Realize also that fixed or administered exchange rates enable the domestic economy to be cushioned from changes in the international economy. If global oil prices change, with flexible exchange rates, there should be immediate changes in the price at which I buy petrol from my neighbourhood petrol pump. There is greater risk and uncertainty, including exposure to foreign exchange risk by companies. There must therefore be adequate instruments to hedge or avoid such risk.

Over-valuation also leads to capital flight. There is bound to be under-invoicing of exports or over-invoicing of imports, so that the money can be stashed abroad. No firm figures exist, but you will hear estimates of 100 billion US dollars illegally stashed abroad. There is no means of testing whether this figure is true or not. But quite clearly, with a realistic exchange rate in the 1990s, reversal of capital flight has taken place. If anything, there is over-invoicing of exports and under-invoicing of imports now. The former is driven by a motive of obtaining duty drawback type concessions or getting income tax concessions. The latter is driven by a motive of paying lower duties.

When the domestic currency's value is reduced under a fixed exchange rate regime, that is known as devaluation. When the domestic currency's value is increased under a fixed exchange rate regime, that's known as revaluation, although this term is rarely used. When the domestic currency's value is reduced under a floating exchange rate regime, that's known as depreciation. When the domestic currency's value is increased under a floating exchange rate regime, that's known as appreciation. Understandably, depreciation and appreciation happen continuously and the changes are incremental. Understandably again, devaluation and revaluation happen at less frequent intervals and the sizes of the changes are larger.

People get very upset about devaluation. They somehow think national pride is at stake if the domestic currency is devalued. The exchange rate has everything to do with price. It should have nothing to do with pride. Because of what I have said earlier, devaluation or depreciation makes India's exports cheaper in foreign currency terms and should therefore increase exports. By how much exports increase is a function of how responsive exports are to price changes and this is captured by the economist's notion of what is called elasticity. Stated simply, it is the percentage change in demand following a percentage change in price. There is a never-ending debate in India about how price elastic India's exports are. Common sense suggests that India's exports should indeed be price elastic. After all, there is little product differentiation and branding, things that reduce the importance of the price factor. We are generally stuck in low value export segments that are price sensitive. Empirical evidence also suggests that India's exports react favourably to devaluation or depreciation, not immediately, but with a time lag of around 18 months. This happened between 1950-51 and 1951-52, following the 1949 devaluation. It happened again between 1972-73 and 1976-77 (following the 1966 devaluation) and between 1978-79 and 1979-80 (when the rupee depreciated). Similarly export growth periods from 1987-88 to 1989-90, 1993-94 to 1995-96 and 1999-2000 to 2001-02 were periods of depreciation. In fact, now there is concern about an appreciating rupee affecting exports adversely.

But simultaneously with depreciation or devaluation, the rupee cost of imported items increases and this triggers inflation. This is one reason why there is some resistance to depreciation or devaluation.

When exchange rate determination is left to the market, there are two broad kinds of theories that try to explain what the exchange rate will be. The first is called purchasing power parity (PPP) and should be interpreted more as an indication of what the exchange rate should be rather than what it actually is. The argument is something like the following. Suppose the inflation rate in India is 6 per cent and that in the rest of the world is 2 per cent. The differential rate of inflation is then 4 per cent and the Indian rupee should (not will) depreciate by 4 per cent to ensure that India's exports remain competitive. Thus, there are notions of the nominal exchange rate and the real exchange rate. The nominal exchange rate is what the exchange rate is today, for instance, Rs. 45.5 to 1 US dollar. The real exchange rate is the nominal exchange rate after adjusting for inflationary trends. Since there are many countries in the world, to obtain an idea of what is happening to the real value of the rupee, one needs to weight and aggregate real rupee movements for all these countries. Some countries are unimportant, so one might as well do this only for the important ones.

Accordingly, the RBI brings out two such indices – a 5-country (USA, Japan, UK, Germany, France) index and a 10-country (in addition to those 5 countries, Netherlands, Italy, Belgium, Switzerland, Australia). Let's use the 10-country index to understand what happens. In 1991-92, the value of the 10-country nominal exchange rate index was 142.40 and in 2001-02, it was 83.49. The rupee has depreciated, as indeed we know it has. But in 1991-92, the value of the 10-country real index was 105.57 and in 2001-02, it was 105.84. The levels are more or less the same. The nominal value of the rupee has depreciated, but more or less in line with the differential rate of inflation. As I said earlier, people worry about PPP when they are concerned about competitiveness of India's exports or about the current account.

The second school of thought focuses on interest rate differentials. If the interest rate in India is 10 per cent and if the interest rate in the US is 2 per cent, people will want to invest their funds in India. This will increase the demand for rupees, lower the demand for dollars and thus lead to the rupee appreciating against the US dollar. It is quite possible for the PPP and interest rate effects to work against each other. Indeed today, interest rates are such that there is an arbitrage possibility of around 3 percentage points, meaning, you can borrow in the US, invest in India and still make 3 per cent. That is part of the reason for India's burgeoning foreign exchange reserves. And it is also the case that the two effects are working against each other in India. Given excess supply of dollars, there is upward pressure on the rupee. And to ensure export growth, we want the rupee to depreciate.

Forex Reserves

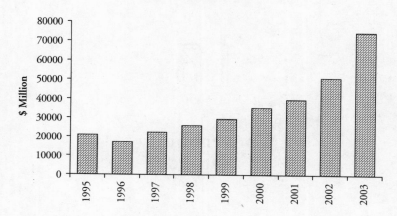

Source: Monthly Economic Report, Dec. 2002, Ministry of Finance

13

Convertibility

INDIA'S foreign exchange reserves are now more than 100 billion US dollars. There is also a term known as foreign currency assets and the expressions foreign exchange reserves and foreign exchange assets are often used synonymously. Actually, they are different. Foreign exchange assets are what are actually held in the form of foreign exchange. In addition, every Central Bank and this includes the RBI, has holdings in the form of gold and SDRs (special drawing rights). SDRs are like international currency, except that they are not used by ordinary people. They were floated by the IMF and are used for settling transactions between countries. When one adds gold and SDR holdings to foreign exchange assets, we have foreign exchange reserves. Of course, the major chunk of what RBI holds as foreign exchange reserves is in the form of foreign exchange assets. Gold and SDR holdings are around 4 billion US dollars. Let's say we have 96 billion US dollars worth of assets.

By any count, this is excessive. Remember that these foreign exchange assets can only be invested in safe investments, which yield a return of marginally less than 3 per cent. There are three reasons why foreign exchange assets have been accumulating, apart of course from export growth and surpluses in the current account. First, like the point made about external debt, assets are held in many different currencies and these are converted into the common numeraire of the US dollar for purposes of comparison. Whenever the US dollar depreciates against other currencies, as it has been doing now, the nominal value of foreign exchange assets increases. Second, there is the arbitrage factor, which I mentioned earlier. Third, the value of the rupee is not entirely determined in the market, meaning, there is intervention by the Central Bank. In exchange rate changes, there is a secular trend over time and there is some volatility around that trend. The RBI intervenes to reduce that volatility, but let's ignore that. However, there is also a secular trend. Given excess supply of dollars, the secular trend will be one of the rupee appreciating against the US dollar and this will hurt exports. In general, the RBI has intervened to buy dollars to ensure the rupee doesn't appreciate in nominal terms. However, there has been some exception to this trend in recent months.

If the RBI buys up dollars from the market, it has to release an equivalent amount of rupees into the system. This is bad for inflation. There is therefore a limit to what the RBI can continue to do in terms of buying up dollars, quite apart from the fact that these reserves only fetch a return of 3 per cent and have built up by offering NRIs (non-resident Indians) returns in excess of 10 per cent. Hence, there is a policy question. What does the RBI do? Should it leave things to the market and allow the rupee to appreciate against the US dollars?

Of course, the government can introduce more liberalization in the external sector to stimulate the demand for dollars. Remove the removing quantitative restrictions on imports. Reduce tariffs. However, since there is a process of WTO negotiations going on, the government would presumably not like to pre-empt the process. That leaves further liberalization of the exchange rate regime.

There is a superficial impression that in the process of reforms, the rupee became convertible on the trade account. Next it became convertible on the current account. And we are waiting for the rupee to now become convertible on the capital account. This superficial impression is incorrect. To the ordinary person, convertibility means something very simple. A currency is convertible when it can be freely converted into a foreign currency and vice-versa. I can walk into a bank and say, here are my rupees. Give me dollars. Or somewhat more unlikely, here are my dollars. Give me rupees. Very few countries in the world have completely convertible currencies in this sense. All countries have some restriction or the other, depending on the kind of transaction. Actually, the IMF defines a convertible currency as one that is convertible on the current account. A currency does not have to be convertible on the capital account for it to be recognized as a convertible currency by the IMF, although there are some moves to change this.

The rupee is not yet completely convertible on the trade account, meaning there continue to be some restrictions. Nor is the rupee completely convertible on the current account, there continue to be some restrictions. Nor is it correct to state that the rupee is not convertible on the capital account. After all, there are very few restrictions on capital inflows. Whatever restrictions remain, exist for capital outflows. That's the reason I said that this notion of neat transition from trade account convertibility to current account convertibility to capital account convertibility is somewhat simplistic. Instead, we are talking about progressive liberalization. Complete convertibility will mean that, as an individual, I can get dollars to invest in the New York stock market. I can get dollars to buy real estate in London. That kind of convertibility will take a long time to come. A few years ago, a committee known as the Tarapore Committee was formed to draw up a roadmap for complete capital account convertibility. That Committee set pre-requisite conditions on capital account convertibility, such as on fiscal deficits and interest rates, that will take at least 10 years to accomplish. That complete capital account convertibility will therefore take many years. Instead, one can have gradual liberalization, if not for individuals, at least for the corporate sector. That's the kind of thing that has happened in the last year. Unfortunately, the recommendations of the Tarapore Committee more or less coincided with the East Asian currency crisis in 1997. From the East Asian crisis, people mistakenly deduced that capital account convertibility was an error and movements towards greater exchange regime liberalization got postponed.

FEMA, which I mentioned earlier, allows for current account convertibility, but capital account controls. I don't think that's the way to look at it. It is very easy to disguise capital account transactions as current account transactions. Even if one is not deliberately trying to indulge in fraud, sometimes, it is very difficult to distinguish the capital account from the current account. Instead, we should have a threshold. No clearances below that, regardless of the nature of the transaction. And clearances above it.

14

External Sector Successes

I began by dividing reforms into a domestic component and an external sector component. I also said that unlike domestic reforms, most reforms in the external sector have either been introduced or there is a clear time frame for their further introduction. I will talk about domestic reforms later. But if external sector reforms have been introduced, have they been successful? The answer will depend on the yardstick one uses to measure success. But my submission is that regardless of which yardstick or indicator you use, the conclusion will be that reforms in the external sector have been outstandingly successful.

Let's take exports first and let us ask a simple question. In how many instances since 1947 has the rupee value of exports increased by more than 10 per cent in three successive years? The answer is 1972-73 to 1976-77, 1981-82 to 1984-85 and 1986-87 to 1996-97. 1990-91 to 1999-2000 is the decade of reforms. In this decade, exports in rupee terms increased by more than 10 per cent in 8 years. They also increased by more than 10 per cent in rupee terms in 2000-01, 2002-03 and look well set to do this in 2003-04 as well. In the 1950s, such increases occurred in 4 years, in the 1960s in 2 years, in the 1970s in 6 years and in the 1980s in 8 years. So if growth in the rupee value of exports is an indicator, the reforms have done exceedingly well.

Let's now ask the same question using the dollar value of exports as an indicator. Exports increased by more than 10 per cent in dollar terms in three successive years between 1972-73 and 1976-77, 1987-88 and 1989-90 and 1993-94 and 1995-96. They also increased by more than 10 per cent in dollar terms in 1999-2000, 2000-01, 2002-03 and look set to do this in 2003-04 as well. There should therefore be no argument that exports have done well. India's share in world exports has also inched up from something like 0.5 per cent to something like 0.8 per cent. Remember also that there was an exogenously imposed shock for part of this time. The East European market, including the Soviet Union, which accounted for almost 20 per cent of India's exports at one point of time, completely evaporated and took some time to revive. The rupee payment system, which characterized trade with these countries and also offered a cushioned market, also disappeared.

India's Foreign Trade

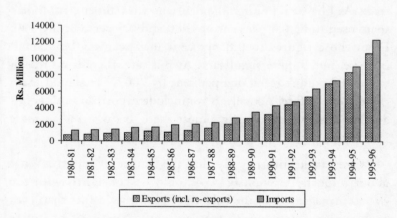

Source: Ministry of Commerce and Industry

However, when talking about exports and imports a point needs to be made. Export data come from two sources. The first source is the Directorate General of Commercial Intelligence & Statistics (DGCI&S) and these figures are also used by Commerce Ministry. These figures are on customs basis. Not all exports and imports go through customs. For instance, most service exports, including software, have no customs angle. They don't figure in DGCI&S data. DGCI&S or Commerce Ministry data are only for merchandise trade. The second source of export and import data is from RBI. This comes on payments basis and includes everything. Thus, Commerce Ministry data under-estimate both exports and imports. The figures I have given above are from Commerce Ministry sources. Since software exports have been doing so well, the growth rate in exports is even more spectacular if you talk about increase in exports of goods and services and not just export of goods.

Commerce Ministry has a target of India attaining one per cent share of world exports by 2007. This is for merchandise trade. As I have said earlier, the figure now is 0.8 per cent. India's share used to be 0.4 per cent in 1980 and 0.5 per cent in 1990. From those figures to 0.8 per cent may seem to be a small increase, but is quite significant. At this rate, there is no reason why we shouldn't reach one per cent by 2007. We should reach there much before. Actually, if we include exports of both goods and services, we are already almost there, because India's share is 0.9 per cent.

One can legitimately say that this is true of exports. What about imports? Obviously, we should be concerned with the overall management of the balance of payments, rather than with exports alone. Between 25 per cent and 30 per cent of India's imports consist of crude oil and the share depends on what is happening to global prices of oil. If we didn't have this oil problem, we wouldn't have a trade deficit either. One way of comparing exports and imports together is to look at what is called the coverage ratio. This is exports divided by imports and therefore measures how much of imports can be paid through exports. This coverage ratio was 66.2 per cent and 75.8 per cent in 2000-01. Again a clear improvement. An alternative is to look at the trade deficit as a percentage of GDP (gross domestic product). This was 3 per cent in 1990-91 and 3.1 per cent in 2000-01. No remarkable change there.

The remarkable change is in what has happened to the current account, which includes the trade account plus invisibles. A large chunk of invisible receipts is what has come in through software exports. Even more remarkable has been the explosion of private transfer receipts, on an average of 10 billion US dollars a year. I personally think this also represents reversal of capital flight thanks to a realistic exchange rate. The net result is that the current account deficit was 3.1 per cent of GDP in 1990-91 and between 1 and 1.5 per cent in the 1990s. Even more interestingly, we have had a current account surplus since 2001-02, although this may change in 2003-04. This is unheard of in India.

That leaves the capital account and I have already talked about improvement in external debt indicators and FDI earlier. A message of the 1990s has gone completely unnoticed. Here is a country that was plagued by a foreign exchange shortage since 1947. This country now has an excess of foreign exchange. It has virtually refused to accept any foreign aid and has become a net lender to the IMF. Apart from specific projects, foreign aid is now important only when donors deal directly with States. Not otherwise. I think this represents a very important change in the mindset also. Just as the Green Revolution eliminated the food constraint, the external sector reforms of the 1990s have eliminated the foreign exchange constraint. This success needs to be appreciated much more.

In the pages that follow, I will turn to domestic reforms, where success has been much more limited.

15

The Constitution

FROM the external sector, let us now turn to the domestic economy. Despite the reforms, the Indian economy is still essentially an insulated one. Exports account for slightly more than 10 per cent of GDP (gross domestic product). Imports account for slightly more than 12 per cent of GDP. Therefore, external sector reforms don't directly affect much of the population. Debate, vested interests and the political economy of reforms accordingly characterize the domestic economy much more. It is not surprising that domestic economic reforms have been tardy.

Whatever be the issue, whatever be the debate, I think the fundamental issue boils down to something very simple. In a country like India, what do we expect the State (the government) to do? Despite a decade of reforms, I don't think we have satisfactorily resolved this issue. Hence the debate about various reforms goes on.

Let me tell you what I think the State should do. I think it is the responsibility of the State to provide a facilitating environment so that individual entrepreneurship can flourish. This doesn't of course mean a complete abolition of the State's regulatory role. I think the State should ensure rule of law and protection of property rights. And I also think the State has a role to play in ensuring some physical and social infrastructure. This is a minimal set of what I expect the State to do. If the State cannot satisfactorily accomplish this minimal set of tasks, there is no point asking the State to do twenty different things. It will end up doing nothing satisfactorily.

That the Indian State is burdened with so many tasks is partly due to the Constitution. The Constitution was adopted in 1949 (formally in 1950). Actually, adopted is the wrong word. We, the people of India, gave ourselves the Constitution. "We, the people of India... hereby adopt, enact and give to ourselves this Constitution." The 1949-1950 Constitution didn't stay unchanged. It has been amended several times. One of these amendments was in 1976-1977. A country that was sovereign and democratic according to the Preamble, became sovereign, socialist, secular and democratic. My lawyer friends tell me that according to the Supreme Court, the basic structure of the Constitution cannot be altered. If this is not a change in the basic structure of the Constitution, I don't know what constitutes a basic change.

I am objecting to use of the word socialism, because no one knows what this word means. If I take up any text-book of economics, it will tell me that socialism means public ownership of the means of production. Public ownership of the means of production doesn't necessarily mean State ownership, although these two distinct notions are often equated. Means of production are inputs that are used to produce outputs. They are also called factors of production.

Any economist says that there are four means of production or inputs – land, labour, capital and entrepreneurship. There have been attempts to publicly own land in several socialist countries. One can't say those experiments have been successful. Apart from a brief experiment in Chinese communes, there have been no experiments to publicly own labour. Doesn't work. So public ownership of means of production is equated with public ownership of capital. I have an even greater problem with entrepreneurship. Entrepreneurship is the business of taking risk. It is the most important input and it is the input that economists understand the least. There are theories of land, labour and capital. You will find hardly any theories about entrepreneurship. Without entrepreneurship, none of the other inputs will work. There won't be any economic activity. And entrepreneurship is fundamentally individual in character. You can't publicly own it.

You may argue that socialism has nothing to do with all this. Socialism everywhere has been associated with notions of equity. That is what we are after and that is the reason we are talking about public ownership of capital. Isn't that what the Constitution says in Article 39(C)? "The State shall, in particular, direct its policy towards securing that the operation of the economic system does not result in the concentration of wealth and means of production to the common detriment." Common detriment is a deliciously vague expression. But let's accept it. So the emphasis is on equity and reducing inequality.

Let's talk now about inequality and I want to make a point now that is important. And it is a point that never fails to upset people. There are two completely different notions of equity and they are distinct. The first notion of equity is an absolute one. An example is the poverty line. I want to ensure that every Indian citizen is above a defined poverty line. That's an absolute notion of equity. I want to ensure that everyone has minimal access to education and health-care. The second notion of equity is a relative one and has to do with inequality. I am interested in a poor person's position relative to a rich man's position. While the absolute notion is indeed important, why are we so concerned with the relative notion of inequality? Why must that be reduced? Let's take an example. In one situation, my monthly income is Rs. 5,000 and yours is Rs. 10,000. In the second situation, my monthly income is Rs. 10,000 and yours is Rs. 50,000. Whatever measure of inequality we use (and there are several), it should be clear that inequality is greater in the second case. But does that mean the second outcome is inferior to the first? I think not, because in the second instance, both our absolute standards have gone up. We should be concerned with absolute notions of equity, not relative ones.

Besides, inequality in what? There is a difference between opportunities and outcome and income is an outcome. If you say that we should reduce inequality in access to education or health-care, I accept the proposition. But why should everyone's income be the same? That's like saying that in an educational institute, everyone must get the same marks, as opposed to arguing that everyone must have equal access to that educational institution. Think about it. And when you think, think with your brain, not with your heart. Too many of our problems result from thinking with the heart.

16

Constitutional Reforms

I think Constitutional reform is essential if we want to get reforms going. The Constitution is a touchstone used by Courts to evaluate policy and we longer have the Constitution we inherited in 1950. I am not a lawyer. Nor am I a Constitutional expert. But here are my common sense comments on what I think we should do with the Constitution.

No one knows what the word "socialism" means, despite everyone swearing by it. Why can't we have a Preamble that doesn't use this word, as was the case before 1976-77? The problem with this Preamble is that because of amendments to the Representation of the People Act, no political party can be registered in India unless it swears by socialism. Obviously, we don't need Articles 6 and 7 any more. These are on "rights of citizenship of certain persons who have migrated to India from Pakistan" and "rights of citizenship of certain migrants to Pakistan". Article 12 is a major one, because it imposes all kinds of social obligations on the "State". Right now, Article 12 states, "In this Part, unless the context otherwise requires, "the State" includes the Government and Parliament of India and the Government and the Legislature of each of the States and all local or other authorities within the territory of India or under the control of the Government of India." The problem is with "under the control" part and this can simply be removed. Under the hypothesis that we revert to 1950, we should clearly bring back the right to property as a fundamental right and restore Article 19(f). Article 24 needs some rewording. At present, it prohibits employment of children under fourteen in factories, mines or hazardous employment. The rewording is necessary because factories have a very specific connotation under the Factories Act.

Even though this is contentious, I think Articles 31A, 31B and 31C should be scrapped. Why should there be laws (such as the Ninth Schedule) that can't be questioned? Articles 36 through 51 are part of the Directive Principles of State Policy and are therefore not judicially enforceable. But unfortunately, such Articles colour many judicial pronouncements. Consider Article 38(2), which says, "The State shall, in particular, strive to minimize the inequalities in income, and endeavour to eliminate inequalities in status, facilities and opportunities, not only amongst individuals but also amongst groups of people residing in different areas or engaged in different vocations." Similarly, Article 39 requires the State to ensure "that the ownership and control of the material resources of the community are so distributed as best to subserve the common good" and "that the operation of the economic system does not result in the concentration of wealth and means of production to the common detriment". Article 40 only mentions village *panchayat*s. Perhaps urban local bodies also require explicit mention.

Hasn't Article 45 become a bit of a joke? This says, "The State shall endeavour to provide, within a period of ten years from the commencement of this Constitution, for free and compulsory education for all children until they complete the age of fourteen years." Articles 47 and 48 also seem outdated and dysfunctional. Article 47 says, "The State shall regard the raising of the level of nutrition and the standard of living of its people and the improvement of public health as among its primary duties and, in particular, the State shall endeavour to bring about prohibition of the consumption except for medicinal purposes of intoxicating drinks and of drugs which are injurious to health." I am objecting to the second half of Article 47, not the first half. As for Article 48, I am objecting to all of it. This says, "The State shall endeavour to organize agriculture and animal husbandry on modern and scientific lines and shall, in particular, take steps for preserving and improving the breeds, and prohibiting the slaughter, of cows and calves and other milch and draught cattle." Certainly on the first half of Article 48, the State should have better things to do.

This takes one to Article 112, on the annual financial statement and expenditure sanctioned out of the Consolidated Fund. Clearly, the idea of the Consolidated Fund, as it stands now, is unworkable. Is there any point in making the distinction between a revenue account and other expenditure? Of course, the problem is not just with expenditure, but receipts also and this takes us to Article 266. Perhaps one should splice Articles 112 and 266 together and link them up with Articles 292 and 293, which deal with borrowing by the Centre and the State governments. There have been suggestions that a cap on the fiscal deficit or government debt (both as shares of GDP) be laid down in the Constitution. That can only be done if these articles are taken in conjunction.

Article 148 recognizes the Comptroller and Auditor General of India (CAG) as a Constitutional authority. There are other regulatory authorities as well. Why shouldn't they be recognized as well?

Article 246 is a major one, since it is linked to a revamping of the Seventh Schedule. Why do we need a Concurrent List any more? Surely a Union List, a State list and a Local Body list should suffice. Obviously, this review should take into account the increasing importance of the services sector and the Seventh Schedule review has to be linked to Article 248, which gives the Centre residuary powers, including the power to tax. This has natural relevance to a VAT (value added tax). Article 261 talks about public acts, records and judicial proceedings. This is the right place to plug in the idea of citizens' right to information. Articles 268 through 281 need complete revamp and recommendations of Finance Commissions can be made mandatory.

Since I am running out of words now and don't want to make this chapter too long, let me be telegraphic now. Scrap Articles 287 and 288. Scrap Article 305. Change Article 311. Redo Article 324. Review Article 356. Discipline Article 368. Scrap Articles 370 and 371.

A review may be controversial and I may also have been simplistic. But I don't think a review is that difficult. But it is necessary.

17

The Legal Framework
and Old Laws

B Y bringing in the Constitution, I have brought in the law.
The legal framework is part of the institutional setup.
Without changes in the institutional setup, I don't see how
reforms can get off the ground. But I also think that economists
often fail to recognize the importance of the law. There are
indeed exceptions, such as in the infrastructure sector. Every
economist will recognize that *the Indian Electricity Act* of 1910
or *the Electricity (Supply) Act* of 1948 needs changes. Or that
FERA became dysfunctional. Or perhaps indeed the need for
changing laws on intellectual property. However, beyond that,
I think there is a lack of appreciation. Partly this has to do with
the non-development of a law and economics discipline in India.
Lawyers don't normally talk to economists. Economists normally
don't talk to lawyers. However, let me not digress too much and
let's get back to the issue of law reform.

Talking about law reform in India is a bit like the story of the
blind men and the elephant. There are six separate issues that one
can list, although these are not water-tight compartmentalizations.
I will talk about the first issue, that of old statutes, in this
chapter. The other issues will follow in subsequent chapters.

But before that, how many statutes are there in India? This is a difficult question to answer. In a federal polity, under Article 246 of the Constitution, there is a Union List, a State List and a Concurrent List. Thus, the Centre and the States can both legislate. There are around 3000 Central statues, around 450 of which deal directly or indirectly with economic and commercial decision-making. The earliest Central statute that continues to be on the statute books is *the Bengal Districts Act*, passed in 1836. The State of Orissa has 1015 statutes, precise figures are impossible to obtain for most States. But generalizing on the basis of the state of Orissa, there must be at least 30,000 State-level statutes. Of course, not all law is statutory in nature. There is a common law tradition, there is case law and some of Constitutional law is different in character.

To come back to the point, many extant statutes in India were passed by the British in the period following the Sepoy Mutiny of 1857. So the first element of legal reform concerns old and dysfunctional laws. These need to be scrapped. India does not have a system of desuetude. Desuetude means that laws are close-ended. This simply means that if a statute is not enforced for a long enough time, courts will regard that this statute has no legal effect. This is even if the statute is not specifically repealed. But unlike Roman or Scots law, this is not accepted as a principle of English law, a tradition that India also follows. There is no desuetude. Therefore, unless a statute is specifically repealed, it continues to be on the statute books. The system is completely open-ended. Unnecessary statutes do not die a natural death and continue on the statute books unless they are lopped off. Dysfunctional statutes are eliminated on an ad hoc basis when the Law Commission prepares reports identifying such statutes and the recommendations are accepted by the government. It would make sense to introduce a system of desuetude. Such dysfunctional statutes also include those that grant monopoly status to public utilities and some statutory reform concerns the removal of government monopolies in public utilities. At the Central government level, several committees have identified such old laws or old sections in laws and around 300 have been junked. But much more needs to be done and very little has happened at the State-level.

An obvious question to ask is, what harm do such old statutes do? There are such old laws in other countries also. For example, taxi-cabs in London are still governed by ancient hackney carriage acts. So taxi-cabs in London must carry enough hay for the horses. No one bothers. The problem is that in India, such old laws are used to harass people. For instance, we have *the Sarais Act* of 1867. *Sarais* are road-side wells and *sarai*-keepers have to offer passers-by free drinks of water under the law. A hotel in Delhi refused to give a bribe and was prosecuted under *the Sarais Act* because it wasn't giving passers-by free drinks of water. Better sense eventually prevailed. But the point is that such old laws provide avenues for discretionary abuse. Why have them?

I can go on and on about old laws. I wrote an entire book about old laws three years ago. Let me not repeat what was in that book. If you think of crime, chances are pretty high that you will think of *the Indian Penal Code (IPC)* of 1860, an unifying and harmonizing statute for which Lord Macaulay should obtain much of the credit. Let me only give you a few sections from IPC and ask you to consider if we should still have these. This is a sample, there are many more.

Section 125 states, "Whoever wages war against the Government of any Asiatic Power in alliance or at peace with the Government of India or attempts to wage such war, or abets the waging of such war, shall be punished with imprisonment for life, to which fine may be added, or with imprisonment of either description for a term which may extend to seven years, to which fine may be added, or with fine." What is an Asiatic power?

Do we need Sections 310 and 311, borrowed originally from *the Thugee Act* of 1836? Section 310 states, "Whoever, at any time after the passing of this Act, shall have been habitually associated with any other or others for the purpose of committing robbery or child-stealing by means of or accompanied with murder, is a thug." Section 311 states, "Whoever is a thug shall be punished with imprisonment for life, and shall also be liable to fine."

Notice also Section 497, a section on adultery. "Whoever has sexual intercourse with a person who is and whom he knows or has reason to believe to be the wife of another man, without the consent or connivance of that man, such sexual intercourse not amounting to the offence of rape, is guilty of the offence of adultery, and shall be punished with imprisonment of either description for a term which may extend to five years, or with fine, or with both. In such case the wife shall not be punishable as an abettor." Notice that the crime of adultery is committed against the man. The woman is the husband's property.

18

Statutory Law Reform

IN the last pages I talked about legal reform and the need to eliminate old statutes. That was the first element of law reform. Let me now turn to other ingredients of statutory law reform.

Second, despite the existence of thousands of statutes on statute books, there are areas where the necessary legislation does not exist today. An example can be hire purchase and leasing. Alternatively, satisfactory exit provisions don't exist for small-scale industry. Let us accept that free entry and exit are integral parts of competition. With competition, there will therefore be exit. That's desirable and can't be postponed indefinitely. We must therefore have satisfactory provisions for exit. The law must evolve so that such gaps are removed.

Third, there are issues of unification and harmonization. Statutes have been enacted at various points in time in the same area. Labour legislation is a case in point. In the field of labour legislation, there are 47 different Central Acts that directly deal with labour. There are many more that indirectly deal with labour. Among the 47 Central Acts, *the Fatal Accidents Act* was enacted in 1855 and *the Public Liability Insurance Act* was enacted in 1991. Given this time span, it stands to reason that concepts and definitions will disagree. For example, there is lack of unanimity about definitions of wages, workman, employee, factory, industry and child labour. Case law also differs, causing further confusion. Banking law is another example of such law of harmonization. There is thus a case for unifying and harmonizing laws.

Fourth, there is an issue of over-legislation. India is a country that is over-legislated and under-governed. Over-legislation is correlated with the problem of reducing unnecessary State intervention. Let me choose *the Essential Commodities Act (ECA)* of 1955 to illustrate what I mean, although I can give you several such examples. ECA didn't stay unaltered since 1955. Over a period of time, it was tightened up more and more. Actually, ECA was originally enacted during a period of wartime shortages, under *the Defence of India Rules* of 1939, and the original *Essential Supplies (Temporary Powers) Act* of 1946 should have died a natural death after wartime shortages were over. Instead, its life was unnaturally prolonged and it permanently entered the statute books in 1955. And through successive amendments in 1964, 1966, 1967, 1971, 1974 and 1981, the government's powers were increased more and more. Let me give you the definition of essential commodity, until ECA was recently amended. Essential commodity means "(i) cattle fodder, including oilcakes and other concentrates; (ii) coal, including coke and other derivatives; (iii) component parts and accessories of automobiles; (iv) cotton and woollen textiles; (iv-a) drugs; (v) foodstuffs, including edible oilseeds and oils; (vi) iron and steel, including manufactured products of iron and steel; (vii) paper, including newsprint, paperboard and straw board; (viii) petroleum and petroleum and other products; (ix) raw cotton, whether ginned or unginned, and cotton seed; (x) raw jute; (xi) any other class of commodity which the Central Government may, by notified order, declare to be an essential commodity". Are all such commodities still plagued by shortages?

What we did was quite simple. Introduce licensing. That creates artificial shortages. With shortages, prices will rise. To prevent price rises, we must have laws like ECA that control production, marketing, storage and distribution. We must have price controls. Isn't it more rational to remove the licensing that caused shortages in the first place?

Fifth, there is the question of administrative law. The word law is used in a narrow sense, as well as in a broad sense. In a narrow sense, law means the aggregate body of statutes. Not all of law is however statutory in nature. Large chunks emanate from a common law tradition and from case law. There are also orders, regulations and procedures, which are not a part of statutory law, but are sanctioned by legislation. Many problems with the law relate not to statutory law, but to these regulations and procedures. Often, regulations and procedures leave a lot of discretion at the petty functionary level. This leads to abuse and has a bearing on some forms of corruption. Let me give examples to illustrate what I mean. *The Factories Act* was passed in 1948 and among other things, requires factories to comply with certain standards. But under *the Factories Act* of 1948, rules have also been enacted. What do these rules say? Every factory must be whitewashed, distemper will not do. So if you are a factory-owner and have distemper, you are violating the law. Every factory must have red-coloured buckets filled with sand, in case there is a fire. Fire extinguishers will not do. Every factory must have earthen pots filled with water for drinking water. Water-coolers will not do. So inspectors descend on you and because you are technically violating the law, there will be a system of bribes and corruption. All machinery requires oil and grease and the government machinery of inspectors is no different. Did you know that under various *Shops and Establishments Acts* and their rules, call centers are technically illegal because they employ people at unearthly hours?

Most of this administrative law is a State-government subject and constraints entry, functioning and exit for any entrepreneurial venture. While statutory law reform has received some attention, almost nothing has happened on administrative law. We don't even know what the country's administrative law is. In 1998, the Government of India set up a Commission on Review of Administrative Laws. Here is a quote from that report, submitted in September 1998. "The Commission was seriously constrained by the fact that it did not have access to a complete set of subordinate legislation in the form of rules, regulations and administrative instructions, issued under different Central Acts, by individual Ministries and Departments. It appears that the Legislative Department itself did not have such a complete compilation of rules, regulations and procedures issued by the

Ministries.... Another handicap was that the Central Ministries did not have full information about the rules and regulations issued by State Governments." This happens to a government-appointed commission on administrative law reform. The commission did not have access to all the administrative law. Apparently, this was last collated in India in 1966. So how can an individual citizen have access to the administrative law?

I am certain you know the legal maxim – ignorance of the law is no excuse. Unfortunately, you will never know what the law exactly is.

19

Arrears in Courts

THE most important segment of law reform concerns procedural law or the speed of dispute resolution. You will often hear the expression governance these days, although no one cares to define it precisely. An integral component of governance is law and order and maintaining law and order is one of the government's core functions. Rule of law means that individuals with civil disputes must have a forum to resolve these disputes quickly. If it takes 20 years to resolve a land or real estate related dispute, the system is simply not credible. In addition, if a crime is committed against society, the criminal justice system must have adequate means of prosecution and conviction. It is no one's case that India doesn't have enough laws. But it is everyone's case that the Indian legal system is not credible, both on civil law and on criminal law.

Let me give you a quote. "Unless a court can start with a reasonably clean slate, improvement of methods is likely to tantalize only. The existence of a mass of arrears takes the heart out of a Presiding judge. He can hardly be expected to take a strong interest in the preliminaries, when he knows that the hearing of the evidence and the decision will not be by him but by his successor after this transfer. So long as such arrears exist, there is temptation to which many Presiding Officers succumb, to hold back the heavier contested suits and devote attention to the lighter ones. The turnout of decisions in contested suits is thus maintained somewhere near the figure of institution, while the real difficult work is pushed into the background." When do you think this was written? It wasn't written recently. In 1924, a Committee was set up under Justice Rankin to make recommendations about speeding up dispute resolution. This Committee submitted its report in 1925 and what I have just quoted, is from that 1925 report. Nothing has changed. If anything, there has been deterioration.

Committees and committees. In 1949, there was a Justice S.R. Das Committee to examine arrears in High Courts. In 1972, there was a Justice J.C. Shah Committee on overall arrears. In 1986, there was the Satish Chandra Committee. In 1990, there was the first Malimath Committee. In 1950, there was a Judicial Reforms Committee only for Uttar Pradesh. In 1986, the Estimates Committee's report also had suggestions about dispute resolution reform. That apart, since 1955, we have had several reports of the Law Commission. The 14th, 79th, 80th, 120th, 121st and 124th reports of the Law Commission especially touched on the question of arrears. There is no dearth of recommendations. Finally, of course, we have the second Malimath Committee's recommendations from 2003. As I just said, there are recommendations and recommendations. There is nothing new under and the sun. It is a matter of getting the recommendations implemented.

Understandably, most recommendations concern the court system. Because most disputes wind up in court, although that doesn't necessarily have to be the case. There are other ways of settling disputes. You also need to remember that India has almost 10,000 courts – 1 Supreme Court, 18 High Courts, 3150 District Courts, 4814 Munsiff or Magistrate's Courts and 1964 Class II Magistrate's Courts. That apart, there exist Land Tribunals, Industrial Tribunals, Tax Tribunals, Service Tribunals,

Company Law Board, Water Pollution Tribunals and Air Pollution Tribunals.

If you ignore tribunals and quasi-judicial bodies, 23 million cases are stuck in courts. The Supreme Court's contribution is marginal in the backlog. Especially after 1995, the status in the Supreme Court has improved significantly. Computers have been used extensively. Similar cases are bunched together and go before the same bench. Stated in an economist's language, the Supreme Court's productivity has increased. Today, the backlog problem is primarily one that plagues High Courts and lower Courts.

3.2 million cases are stuck in High Courts. That's not the best indication of how bad the situation is. Every year, some new cases are instituted and some old cases are disposed of. If the number of new cases exceeds the ones that are disposed of, the situation gets worse over time and that is indeed the problem with High Courts. Of course, one should mention that there has been some improvement in the 1990s. 1995 seems to be the cutoff year. Till 1994, cases disposed of were between 80 and 85 per cent of new cases. Since 1995, this ratio has been more than 90 per cent. But unless this ratio increases to more than 100 per cent, we won't begin to make a dent on the backlog. Of the 3.2 million cases that are stuck in High Courts, 500,000 cases have been stuck for more than 10 years. Of these, 185,363 cases are in Allahabad High Court and 131,256 cases are in Calcutta High Court. That is, if the Allahabad and Calcutta High Court problems can be resolved, we won't have that many old cases. Other than these High Courts, there are also large backlogs in Chennai, Kerala and Mumbai High Courts. By the way, of the 3.2 million cases stuck in High Courts, 88 per cent are civil cases. Only 12 per cent are criminal cases.

The situation is exactly the opposite in lower Courts. Of the 20 million cases stuck in lower courts, two-thirds are criminal cases. And in general, the conviction rate is lower than 5 per cent. No wonder the Indian legal system has such a terrible reputation. Having said this, we should recognize that there has been some improvement in lower Courts in the 1990s, even if we find that difficult to believe. Today, this kind of backlog is primarily concentrated in UP, Gujarat, Maharashtra, Madhya Pradesh, West Bengal and Karnataka. And so far, improvements have been limited in UP, Maharashtra and Karnataka. Next chapter, I will talk about various methods that are possible to reduce the backlog problem and speed up dispute resolution.

Solving the Arrears Problem

To make the legal system credible, we need to reduce arrears and speed up dispute resolution. At various stages, several recommendations have been made to make this possible and these recommendations can be classified under a number of separate heads.

First, we can try and reduce the demand on court cases. Why must every dispute be dragged to court? There are other ways of settling disputes, often referred to as alternative dispute resolution. Conciliation, mediation and arbitration are other means of settling disputes, alternatives to adjudication through courts. Arbitration is of course for commercial disputes. What is the difference between conciliation and mediation? Sometimes, these two words are used synonymously. If a distinction is actually drawn between conciliation and mediation, it can be something like the following. Conciliation occurs when a third party nips the dispute in the bud and the two disputing parties are brought together. So the dispute is effectively never recognized as a dispute. Mediation occurs when there is a dispute and a third party suggests a compromise solution to settle the dispute. Arbitration is also like that, except the third party in an arbitration dispute has some legal standing. Earlier, this binding aspect of arbitration used to be through *the Arbitration Act* of 1940. Now we have *the Arbitration and Conciliation Act* of 1996.

There are several reasons why these alternative channels have failed to function effectively. Credible conciliators and mediators didn't exist. The British tried to replace everything with the court system and historical forums of alternative dispute resolution simply fell into disuse. There were problems with the 1940 *Arbitration Act.* As a result, with the 1940 law, arbitration was simply a step one had to go through before the dispute was dragged to court. The 1996 version has improved things. Hence, by using alternative channels, we can reduce pressure on the court system.

Second, we can reduce pressure on the court system by getting the government out. Understandably, the government has to be one of the two parties in a criminal dispute. But do you know that in at least 60 per cent of civil disputes, the government is also a party? Sometimes, the government is a party on both sides, meaning two government organizations decide to fight it out using courts. Naturally, courts don't have time for ordinary citizens. In 1994, the State Law Ministers took a decision that whenever there is a dispute between two government organizations, that dispute will be settled outside the court system. As far as I know, that decision hasn't been implemented yet. Many of these government cases also involve appeals. Some studies show that more than 90 per cent of government appeals fail. That is, they are appeals that shouldn't have been made in the first place. Unfortunately, in the government system, it is impossible to punish a government officer who is responsible for pointless appeals. More generally, moving away from the government, we have too many appeals by everyone. In general, the Indian system is that two appeals are permitted, one on grounds of fact and another one on grounds of law. Why do we need two appeals? What is wrong with just one appeal? I doubt that a single appeal system will make the justice delivery system less fair. Finally, on the government, too many government cases involve tax-related litigation. Do you know that the Supreme

Court of the country has at various points in time had to decide whether betel leaves, chilies, lemons, ginger and coconuts are vegetables? That is because vegetables don't pay excise. Surely the Supreme Court, the highest court of the land, should have better things to do. The responsibility for such unnecessary cases doesn't lie with courts. It lies with economists who have foisted an unnecessarily complicated direct and indirect tax structure on the country. Implement the recommendations of the two Kelkar Task Forces on direct and indirect taxes and many cases will disappear.

Third, there is the standard argument that we must have more courts and more judges. That in a way was the idea behind setting up tribunals or Lok Adalats under *the Legal Services Authorities Act* of 1989. In some States, *panchayat*s have been given dispute resolution powers. There are Family Courts and Women's Courts. Since 2001, 1734 fast track courts have also been started. The success of these attempts varies from State to State and forum to forum. Essentially, these alternative forums have the power to evolve their own procedures, distinct from cumbersome court procedures. In instances where such distinct procedures have evolved, success has been better. On more courts and more judges, one should also mention that often there are vacancies for judges. But these are not filled in time. Or sitting judges are dragged away to head commissions of inquiry.

Fourth, even if all these improvements take place, court cases won't disappear. So the efficiency with which courts handle cases must improve. Part of this concerns procedural law. Complicated procedural law causes delays at each of the four steps a civil case goes through – pre-trial, trial, appellate and execution. Interminable verbal arguments, adjournments and so on. The procedural law for civil cases is essentially *the Civil Procedure Code*. Thankfully, this has now been amended and delays in civil cases should drop. However, *the Criminal Procedure Code* (and *the Indian Evidence Act*), relevant for criminal cases, is yet to be amended. Recently, the second Malimath Committee has made drastic recommendations about reforming India's criminal justice system. But reforms will take a long time in coming. I told you earlier, that efficiency in the Supreme Court has increased. Judges are however generally reluctant to impose work norms on themselves. How many holidays are there in a year? Do we still need long summer vacations, a legacy of the raj? How many minutes a day does a judge work? How many judgements are actually written? Increasing judges and courts without addressing such questions will not work.

Notice that I pegged the discussion on law reform to economic reforms. But this pegging is unnecessary. Even if economic reforms hadn't taken place in the 1990s, the legal system would still have needed reform. It was simply not satisfactory. The onset of liberalization merely bolstered the argument.

20

Governance

THE word governance is often used. But it is a term that is not always precisely defined, although several international organizations have tried to define governance and what it covers. Clearly, law and order is an integral part of governance. And the criminal justice system certainly doesn't convey the impression that India is a country that is well governed.

Before talking about criminal justice, we should define what the word crime means. A crime occurs when someone breaks the law and many definitions of crime are linked to *the Indian Penal Code* (IPC). That apart, there are other definitions of crime under what are called Special and Local Laws (SLL). Every year, Ministry of Home Affairs brings out a book titled "Crime in India". That tells us how many people have been prosecuted and convicted for crimes committed under the IPC or SLL. Crimes can also be divided into those that are cognizable and those that are non-cognizable. The police have to investigate cognizable crimes and in general, those accused can be arrested without a warrant. Subject to some simplification, warrants for arrests are required for non-cognizable crimes, obtained from magistrates. Cognizable crimes are more serious.

From "Crime in India" I have data for 2000. And this tells me that 5.17 million cognizable crimes were committed in India. This is for crimes investigated by the police. Crimes investigated by other investigative agencies aren't included in this 5.17 million figure. If you include other investigative agencies, the number of cognizable crimes is 5.24 million. Cognizable crimes conjure up visions of serious crimes like murder, theft, dacoity and rape. "Crime in India" also has a category of "other IPC crimes". These are minor crimes. When I look at the 2000 data, I find that 38.75 per cent of those arrested for IPC violations are under this minor category. Most serious crimes under SLL concern excise violations, gambling and prostitution. But SLL also has a minor "other SLL crimes" category and I find that 69.79 per cent of those arrested for SLL violations were for this minor category. The point I am making is simple. Those who are arrested are poor. Those who are rich never get arrested. Those who deserve to be in jail are outside it and those who are in jail deserve to be outside it. For crimes, the actual rate of conviction is less than 5 per cent. That doesn't make the system of governance credible.

The problem is not just with arrests. The problem is more with what happens thereafter. After all, if you are innocent, you will be acquitted eventually. There is no problem if the Criminal Procedure Code or instructions by courts are strictly observed. The accused will be told what crime he (or she) has been accused of. If the accused doesn't have the money to pay for a lawyer, there will be free legal aid and the free services of a lawyer. In 24 hours, he (or she) will have to be produced before a Magistrate and if the arrest is unwarranted, the accused will be released. In 24 hours, the police will have to decide on the charges. If serious crimes merit longer time periods, there is a provision for police or judicial custody, with the latter preferred. But police custody cannot be for more than 15 days. For bailable offences, bail will be promptly granted and the amount of bail

shouldn't be excessive. If the police cannot produce the charge
sheet in 60 or 90 days, the accused will be promptly released.

Excellent principles. In 1997, a report was prepared for Tihar
Jail in Delhi. This found that 85 per cent of those in Tihar Jail
were under-trials. There was no question of bail, they were
awaiting trial. Most of these were people who were accused of
petty crimes and had been in jail for more than the maximum
mandatory sentences for such crimes. The Tihar Jail figure of 85
per cent is not an exception. Most jails report similar figures.
There are 1200 jails in India. And the jail population is 380,000.
Of which, 280,000 or 74 per cent represent under-trials. And
out of these under-trials, 95 per cent are those who are accused
of petty or minor crimes.

This socialist country, whatever that expression means, is
supposed to represent the interests of the poor. That is certainly
not what happens with the criminal justice system.

To bring about changes in the criminal justice system, we
need not only changes in *the Criminal Procedure Code* and *the
Indian Evidence Act*, but also in the attitudes of the police. Plus
prison or jail reform. To discover what needs to be done, read
two reports. I am not making this up. One committee's report
goes back to 1838, this committee being set up thanks to Lord
Macaulay. The second report goes back to 1919-20. Both of
these concern jail reform. Since nothing much has changed,
those ancient reports will do. Or if you prefer more recent stuff,
there was an All India Committee on Jail Reforms, under the
Chairmanship of Justice Mulla and from 1980-83 vintage.
Reports of the Law Commission or the National Human Rights
Commission have also indicated changes. But since little has
been implemented, the 1894 Prisons Act continues unchanged.

As for the police, here is a quote. "The police force
throughout the country is in a most unsatisfactory condition,
that abuses are common everywhere, that this involves great

injury to the people and discredit to the government, and that radical reforms are required." Guess when this was written. This quote is from the 1902-03 National Police Commission's report. In more recent times, we have had the 1979-81 National Police Commission report, the 1998 Ribeiro Committee report and the 2000 Padmanabhaiah Committee report. No dearth of recommendations. Precious little implementation. No need for fresh recommendations. The 1861 Police Act continues unchanged.

Governance is not just about reforming the criminal justice system or the police. A subset of the governance reform agenda is what may be called administrative reform. This should cover reforms in both the executive and the legislature. But within the executive, civil service reform is an integral part of administrative reform.

21

Administrative Reform

THE Indian administrative structure was created by the British to rule a colony. Driven partly by the motive to collect land revenue, the British created an extremely centralized system of administration, which we inherited, and then perfected. Without decentralization and devolution of decision-making powers, it is impossible to administer a large and heterogeneous country. Perhaps one should mention that the Chinese economy has always been decentralized, even during the days of centralized planning.

The Constitution gives us a Seventh Schedule. According to this, we have a Union List and a State List and of course, a Concurrent List. A reading of the Seventh Schedule will indicate the kind of centralization we have inherited. Most States complain about excessive centralization. By decentralization, they mean decentralization of decision-making from the Centre to the States. Very few States are willing to talk about decentralization within the State, with decision-making devolved from States to local bodies like *panchayat*s and urban local bodies. Article 243 of the Constitution certainly recognizes an Eleventh and a Twelfth Schedule. These Schedules indicate what should be handed down to *panchayati raj* institutions (PRIs) and urban local bodies (ULBs). There is a difference between should be handed down and must be handed down. Consequently, very few States have decentralized decision-making. Yet, what should be done is crystal clear. There should be a complete revamp of the Seventh, Eleventh and Twelfth Schedules. Let there be only three lists – for Centre, State and Local Bodies. No need for Concurrent Lists. This decentralization must be mandatory, no scope for discretion on the part of States. Simultaneously, there must be fiscal devolution. How can you have responsibilities on local bodies without revenue generating powers?

There are several centrally sponsored schemes (CSSs) in India. Most are for poverty alleviation or improving physical infrastructure in rural areas. There is no exact listing of how many CSSs there are. Some say 250. Others say 350. Those who are supposed to administer these programmes have sometimes forgotten that these even exist. Had number of programmes succeeded in removing poverty, we would have removed poverty long ago. Several Planning Commission reports have established that such programmes do little to remove poverty. Don't misunderstand. There has been expenditure. But this expenditure hasn't led to any improvement in outcomes. This is partly related to government budgetary processes and how success is judged within the government system. Success is judged in terms of expenditure. What this expenditure has led to, is not a consideration. The Indira Awaas Yojana seems to be an exception. Because in this case, the Planning Commission estimates that 25 per cent of what has been spent has reached the target beneficiary. For other programmes, the figure is often closer to 5 per cent. Sometimes, people think the leakage of 95 per cent is due to corruption. That's not quite true. There is certainly corruption. But the bulk of the leakage is due to high administrative costs. Why should we have central programmes for poverty alleviation and building social infrastructure? Can't the money be handed over to local bodies? This is not to suggest that there is no corruption at local body levels. Euphoria about local bodies is indeed unwarranted. In many States, there can be valid question marks about what happens in *panchayat*s or *panchayat* elections. Nevertheless, one argument can possibly be accepted. If the number of administrative hierarchies is reduced, leakage should decline.

Let's take a figure. Every year, we spend Rs. 50,000 crores, if not more, on poverty alleviation and rural development. The number of people below the poverty line is not more than 300 million. If this Rs. 50,000 crores was directly transferred to this poor population, each poor individual would get Rs. 1667 a year. With 6 people per poor household, each poor household would get Rs. 10,000 a year. Had this money truly reached the target beneficiary, there would have been no poverty left in India. Similar to the CSS decentralization idea, is the argument about planning. Our planning process emanates from top and percolates down to the bottom. Instead of this, the planning process itself should start from the bottom and move up. After all, planning should involve those for whom we are planning. We should go from the village to the block, from the block to the district, from the district to the State capital, from the State capital to Delhi. Planning is about providing public goods, goods that have positive externalities and should be provided by the State. But each public good is optimally provided at a certain level of government. For instance, national defence is efficiently provided at the level of Centre. But why should the Centre be charged with the responsibility of looking after village ponds?

Right to Information Acts are also linked with accountability and transparency of government expenditure. Some States have these now, often with caveats that nullify the purpose for which these laws were enacted. There was a famous economist named John Maynard Keynes, who wrote some of his influential stuff during the 1920s and the 1930s, a period of depression and unemployment. Keynes argued that with unemployed resources, people should be hired to dig ditches. These ditches were of no use to anyone. So after these ditches had been dug up, people should again be hired to fill them up again. In the process, the economy would be stimulated. Keynes is taught in every college and university in India. Therefore, it is not surprising that we should have improved on his ideas. No need to actually dig the ditches. In government files, you will find countless examples of roads that haven't actually been built. Wells that haven't actually been dug. They only exist on paper, although money has been spent on them. Right to Information Acts, if properly enacted and enforced, can monitor efficiency of government expenditure and make it more transparent and accountable.

Most State governments don't yet have Right to Information Acts. Most government departments don't yet have Citizens' Charters, which also can improve accountability. If the citizen's rights are clearly enunciated, the citizen can expect public services as a matter of right. And demand compensation if these services aren't satisfactorily provided. Some States have experimented successfully, often using the idea of e-governance or electronic governance. When successful, corruption has declined. This links up with the broader idea of civil service reform and making the civil service more accountable. Why should information about transfers, corrupt officers and vigilance enquiries not be in the public domain? The civil service now exists to serve independent Indian citizens. It no longer exists to serve the interests of a foreign colonial power.

22

Corruption

CORRUPTION is always in the news in India. Every now and then, a report emanates from Transparency International (or a similar organization), pointing out that India is one of the most corrupt countries in the world. In Transparency International's 2003 Corruption Perceptions Index, India is ranked 83rd out of 133 possible ranks. (133 is not the number of countries, since many countries share the same rank. India shares the 83rd rank with the likes of Malawi and Romania.) There will be studies that 40 per cent of national income is accounted for by the black or illegal economy. At an anecdotal level, people will give you sociological explanations for corruption. The rulers used to be British. They were alien. Hence, there was some perverse satisfaction in cheating alien rulers. After all, most forms of corruption involve a revenue loss for the government. Others will talk about declining moral values. In good old *Satya Yuga*, people were honest. These are the perils of *Kalyuga*.

Black income is generally estimated to be 40 per cent of GDP (gross domestic product) or national income and this is a figure that almost everyone quotes. I always have a problem with this 40 per cent figure. Most instances of corruption one thinks of are transfer payments for purposes of national income accounting. Hence, they don't affect GDP. People will mention tax evasion, direct or indirect. What segments of the Indian economy are expected to pay taxes, direct or indirect? Primarily the organized sector. And what is an upper bound for the organized sector's contribution to GDP? Not more than 25 per cent, probably closer to 15 per cent. Therefore, I think this 40 per cent figure is an over-estimate, although I have no means of judging what the true figure is.

Despite my obvious biases, I am convinced corruption is economic in nature. There is nothing historical, social or cultural about it. And there are several strands to corruption, although it is not always easy to disentangle them. First, there are petty forms of corruption, similar to bribes one pays for telephone or gas connections. These result from licensing, which leads to shortages. As reforms eliminate licensing and shortages, these forms of corruption will disappear and this has indeed begun to happen for telephone or gas connections.

Second, there is corruption that results from arbitrage opportunities. If the tax rate on domestic sales is 30 per cent, while that on export sales is 0 per cent, there will be in-built incentive for paper exports, that is, domestic sales will masquerade as exports by bribing customs. If branded garments pay excise, while unbranded garments do not, there will be an incentive to bribe excise inspectors so that branded garments masquerade as unbranded ones. If the official exchange rate is 45 dollars to a rupee and this is over-valued, there will be an automatic incentive to boost *hawala* transactions. If there is an unreasonably high import duty on gold, smuggling incentives will also boost *hawala* transactions. The answer to these kinds of corruption is to make direct tax rates reasonable and rationalize and harmonize indirect taxes (including customs, excise and sales tax).

Third, there is corruption that results from too much of discretion at the petty functionary level. Discretion inevitably leads to abuse. As a citizen or businessman, I will not know what the rules are. Rules will be sufficiently non-transparent and vague for interpretation in my favour to be necessary. Hence, a price will be exacted for this favourable interpretation. Some varieties of land or real estate corruption belong to this category. Notice that this kind of corruption is not distributionally neutral. In relative terms, it hurts the poor more than it hurts the rich. The poor are perpetually trying to establish their identity, searching for gazetted officers to sign various pieces of paper. They don't usually have driving licences or passports. They are always bribing to get things done. Why can't we have a national identity card system that will make it easier to identify poor people for subsidies also? Actually, the Kelkar Task Forces do argue for such an I-card system. This kind of corruption is also linked to reforming administrative law, the plethora of rules, regulations and orders. These make every sensible entrepreneurial activity illegal, or subject to licensing. Don't think licensing only affects the rich. Madhu Kishwar has enough material to document corruption faced by rickshaw pullers and street vendors in Delhi. Samuel Paul, in Bangalore, also has similar documentation for all manner of public services. In 1989, Hernando de Soto published a book titled "The Other Path". This documented how the poor in Peru were constrained to live, and earn a living, outside the legal system. India is no different. This idea of reduced discretion and greater transparency can also be extended to government transfers. Money is also made in government jobs through transfers. For instance, I am told that the favoured location for a police inspector in Delhi is Chandni Chowk and the unfavoured location is the VIP circuit in Central and South Delhi. Like Tughlak Road.

Fourth, there is the question of government decisions, especially on procurement. Some defence deals are examples. There is a government procurement code at the WTO (World Trade Organization), but India is not a signatory. Procurement is therefore not necessarily done through global bids. This impinges on electoral reform also, especially electoral funding. I don't think morality and ethics are basic. The basic question is electoral funding. If I invest resources in a venture, I will expect a 15 per cent or 20 per cent rate of return on that venture. Why should the logic be different if I am a politician?

Eventually, reforms should lead to reduced corruption. But as experiences of several other countries have shown, during an interim period of transition, that doesn't necessarily happen. Discretion often increases. Privatization decisions are an example. However, the message should be clear. Reforms eventually reduce corruption. Incidents of corruption should not be used as an excuse for non-reforming.

We can be cynical about this and throw up our hands in despair. Alternatively, there can be an attempt to improve governance. This is where Rudi Guiliani's model in New York has relevance. The idea is to attack the more visible forms of corruption, the smaller ones. Leave out the high-end types to sort themselves out. Mr. Vittal has also been propagating this micro-type endeavour.

The Ig Nobel Lal Bihari

Cadastral surveys bring up Lal Bihari. Have you heard of Ig Nobel Prizes? Indians have higher representation in winning Ig Nobel prizes than Nobel ones. Ig Nobel prizes are awarded for odd achievements or scientific discoveries. In 2002, Marc Abrahams published a book on Ig Nobel prizes and their winners. Take 2002. Sreekumar and G. Nirmalan (Kerala Agricultural University) won it in mathematics for their research on "Estimation of the Total Surface Area in Indian Elephants (Elephas Maximus Indicus)". Evidently, this Sreekumar-Nirmalan technique enables you to estimate an elephant's surface area without actually measuring it. Without linking Lal Bihari to Ig Nobel, I have written about him before. Therefore, when I discovered the year 2003's Ig Nobel peace prize was awarded to

Lal Bihari, I felt a moral obligation to revisit Lal Bihari. And this decision was reinforced when I found that Lal Bihari's web citation has a cross-link to my earlier article.

Who is Lal Bihari? The citation says Lal Bihari, from UP, won the prize for a triple accomplishment: first, for leading an active life even though he has been declared legally dead; second, for waging a lively posthumous campaign against bureaucratic inertia and greedy relatives; and third, for creating the Association of Dead People (*Mritak Sangh*). Lal Bihari couldn't attend the award ceremony in Harvard. Madhu Kapoor received the award of his behalf. And Satish Kaushik (who else?) will soon make a film about Lal Bihari's life and death.

You get the general idea. *Mritak Sangh*'s members are those who have been officially declared dead by relatives, acquisition of the dead person's land being the objective. Once you are declared dead, it is difficult to prove you are alive. Forming an association helps. Several such instances were reported in 1999 and 2000, especially from Azamgarh district in UP and *Mritak Sangh* was formed, with Lal Bihari as the founder. Depending on whom you believe, *Mritak Sangh* has anything between 25 and 10,000 members. Don't misunderstand. This is not the number of living dead. This is the number of *Mritak Sangh* members.

In 1975, Lal Bihari discovered he had been declared dead by his uncle. Had he not applied for a bank loan, he might not have discovered it until much later. It doesn't require much to get a death certificate issued under *the Registration of Births and Deaths Act* of 1969. An application, a medical certificate confirming death, an affidavit and a copy of a ration card (or other proof of identity) of the applicant will do. Technically, the police station is supposed to check before a death certificate is issued. But presumably, corruption takes care of that. Now you need to apply to the land registry office to get land transferred and corruption takes care of that as well. As far as I can make out, *the Registration Act* of 1908 and accompanying rules cover registration of agricultural land and these also provide for penalties for fraudulent registration by Registration Officers. But when are such penalties ever enforced?

How do you prove you are alive, especially if a case is stuck in court for 25 years? Lal Bihari tried publicity - get arrested, stand for Parliament, attract contempt charges by courts, write pamphlets, organize your own funeral, demand a widow's pension for your wife, add the word Mritak to your name. All these would have publicly acknowledged that he existed. It took 19 years, from 1975 to 1994, for him to prove he was alive, thanks to help from the District Magistrate. Having been reincarnated, Lal Bihari became the champion of other living dead, through *Mritak Sangh*.

Nothing much might have happened, had it not been for a report in *Time* magazine in 1999, picked up by newspapers from Australia to Zimbabwe. Allahabad High Court took *suo motu* notice of the *Time* report and Justices Dhawan and Dikshit directed the district administration to pool information on such dead people walking and place it before the district Chief Judicial Magistrate. How do you collect such information? Make announcements through local newspapers and radio so that people declared dead in revenue records approach the *gram pradhan*. This exercise had a timeframe of September 1999. In this limited exercise conducted in Azamgarh district, 80 such dead cases were identified. Thirty dead people were rehabilitated, that is, declared alive. But only around four got their land back. 16 guilty revenue record officials were identified. The High Court wanted them to be criminally prosecuted. How many have been prosecuted and if prosecuted, how many have been punished? I don't know and the answer probably is - none at all.

This doesn't solve the systemic problem. In Azamgarh, under instructions from the High Court, the District Magistrate was given 10 computers to computerize land records. Computerization of land records is high on e-governance initiatives of many States. *Bhoomi* in Karnataka is not the only one. There is AP and now there is Rajasthan. Since 1988-89, there has also been a centrally-sponsored scheme for computerization of land records. Computerization has its uses and makes the search function easier. Therefore, getting certificates of titles becomes faster. And some corruption is eliminated.

But if the original data are wrong, computerization doesn't help. The word cadastral means a survey, for example, of land ownership and can be used for revenue collection. When was the last cadastral survey in India undertaken? I have asked several knowledgeable people and no one has been able to tell me. Everyone agrees no surveys have been done since Independence. The only precise date I have is the 1920s, presumably, for some States. To recheck, I have gone through all the 10 Plan documents and find that each one made this point about cadastral surveys being necessary. For example, the Sixth Plan said, "Systematic programmes would be taken up for compilation/updating of land records for completion within a period of five years, i.e., 1980-1985. In States, where the backlog is heavy, aerial survey techniques may be employed for expeditious survey operations. Each cultivator would be given a passbook indicating his status/title to description of the land - viz., area, cess, etc - along with a copy of khasra/map and other details that are considered necessary. Appropriate provision will be made in revenue laws to confer legal status on these documents as proof of title and rights in land".

This hasn't happened. And Lal Biharis will continue to receive Ig Nobel prizes. The Ig Nobel prizes state, "The winners have all done things that first make people laugh, then make them think." I find it especially poignant that these prizes were awarded on 2nd October. Should make us think.

23

Health, Education and the Government

EVERY citizen has the right to demand certain things from the government. This is a minimal set of demands that the government is expected to deliver on. What is your minimal set of services the government should deliver on? My set is education, health and law and order. If a government satisfactorily delivers on these three, one can try to think of other things the government should do. But if a government cannot successfully deliver on these three core functions, what is the point of asking a government to do twenty other things? It won't satisfactorily deliver on these twenty other items. But in the process, it won't also deliver on the three core items I have mentioned.

India is a socialist country and the question of socialism has occurred before. What is the definition of socialism? Partly, the definition of socialism involves an emphasis on equity and reducing disparities. But every socialist country I can think of, also has a phenomenal record in improving health and education outcomes. And in these two social sector heads, disparities across class, caste and gender are removed. We are a socialist country, but we haven't been able to accomplish this goal. Every year, the

World Bank brings out a document known as World Development Report (WDR) and WDR data can be used to make cross-country comparisons. Take the WDR for 2003 as an example. According to this document, in 2000, India's illiteracy rate was 43 per cent. Forget developed countries. Among developing countries in Asia, I find that China had an illiteracy rate of 16 per cent, Mongolia had an illiteracy rate of 1 per cent and Vietnam had an illiteracy rate of 7 per cent. We can move on to health and the under-five mortality rate (expressed per thousand) is an useful indicator of health conditions. In 2000, the rate was 88 in India. It was 39 in China, 71 in Mongolia and 34 in Vietnam. So we haven't got what socialism delivers. The Indian government hasn't delivered on health and education. I have already talked about law and order earlier.

Yet, every year, the government spends money. I think all government expenditure should be evaluated in terms of whether it improves health, education and law and order or not. Of course, one needs to be slightly careful. Thanks to the basic structure of the Constitution, much of the responsibility for health and education is on the States. Not on the Centre. Nevertheless, let's check to see what the Central government is spending its money on. The 2003-04 budget will be good enough to drive home the point. By the 2003-04 budget, I mean the budget estimates (BE) for 2003-04. There is indeed a problem with government budgetary figures. BE figures are proposals. One year down the line, we get revised estimates (RE) and don't be surprised if RE differs from BE. That's quite normal. One year further down the line, we will get actual figures. And actuals will differ both from RE and BE. That's also quite normal.

As with any household budget, if you subtract expenditure from income or receipts, you get the deficit. When we try to manage household budgets, we realize a simple proposition. If you have a deficit, you will have to increase income or reduce expenditure. The problem is that the government has another option. Using the Central Bank or RBI, the government has the option of printing money. This is not an option available to households. Printing money leads to an increase in inflation. Inflation hurts the rich only marginally. Their incomes are often indexed to inflation rates through things like dearness allowances (DA), even if DA increases take place with a time lag. This is not an option that is available to the poor. Therefore, inflation is a bit like a tax imposed on the poor. More importantly, this is a regressive tax. The rich pay a progressive tax more than proportionately. The poor pay a regressive tax more than proportionately. Inflation is a regressive tax. It hurts the poor relatively more. After reforms started, automatic monetisation of the deficit has ended. But earlier, it used to happen regularly.

Other than printing money or monetisation, yet another way of meeting the deficit is borrowing. That option is also available for household budget management. But there is a difference. A household that borrows knows that it has to eventually pay back the loan. A government also has to eventually pay back the loan. But the difference is that the loan has to be paid back by a future government, not the present one. The fiscal deficit is a measure of how much the government is borrowing in any year. That's the difference between the fiscal deficit and the overall budget deficit. According to BE for 2003-04, the Central government will borrow 153637 crores of rupees in 2003-04. Remember what I said earlier. BE will not necessarily tally with RE or actuals. For instance, BE of 2002-03 told us the Central government would borrow 135524 crores of rupees. Eventually, the government actually borrowed 140955 crores of rupees.

There are two problems with borrowing. First, the borrowing eventually has to be paid. That means this money cannot be used for anything else, such as building physical infrastructure or spending on social infrastructure. Second, you and I are small entities. If you and I borrow, there is no impact on interest rates.

Government borrowing is large. It has an upward pressure on interest rates. That doesn't only impact borrowing by the corporate sector. It also impacts our borrowing, when we borrow as consumers to buy cars or TVs or fridges. If the government borrows at 9.5 per cent, banks also have to offer 9.5 per cent to attract deposits. Naturally, the bank lending rate will be higher than 9.5 per cent. After all, banks are not in this business for charity.

It's not the case that we don't borrow. But we borrow for specific purposes, such as buying cars or financing education or buying houses. These can be regarded as investments, physical or social. Investments are addition to capital and education is nothing but investing in human capital. In other words, borrowing can be justified if assets are created. If the government borrows 153637 crores for investments, not many people will object. The issue then is the use the government makes of the borrowed money.

24

Government Expenses

GOVERNMENT expenses are divided into a revenue account and a capital account. The revenue account is a bit like consumption, it is expenditure needed to meet running expenses. The capital account is a bit like investments, capital expenditure adds to the future productive potential of the economy. Capital expenditure involves the creation of assets. One must of course remember that this division into revenue expenditure and capital expenditure is slightly artificial. Especially if one has the Central government in mind. When the Centre offers grants to State governments, grants that may be used by State governments for capital expenditure, this expenditure will show up in Central government accounts as revenue expenditure. Similarly, if a new asset is being created, that will show up in the Central government's books as capital expenditure. But running or maintaining that new asset is equally important. However, running or maintenance will show up as revenue expenditure. Despite these problems with the revenue cum capital expenditure division, everyone rightly argues that the government should be indulging in capital expenditure. Not revenue expenditure. In general, there will probably be a deficit in the capital account. That needs to be financed through a surplus in the revenue account.

Fair enough. So let us see what our Central government proposes to do in the year 2003-04, as given in the BE (budget estimates). I have already told you that the government proposes to borrow 153637 crores. In 2003-04, the government proposes to spend 438795 crores of rupees. Of this, 366227 crores or 83.46 per cent is on revenue expenditure. 72568 crores or 16.54 per cent is capital expenditure. I have given you figures for 2003-04. But the figures for any other budget are no different. Remember I have already told you that the fiscal deficit, the amount the government borrows, is 153637 crores. And the revenue deficit is Rs. 112292 crores. This is clearly not what is supposed to happen.

People often argue that no one objects to reforms these days. Every political party agrees that the fiscal deficit is high and should be reduced. Every political party agrees that the revenue deficit should be reduced. There is political consensus on this. To me, this is a meaningless consensus. Unless we agree on how the fiscal deficit is to be reduced, the apparent consensus doesn't get us very far. There will be a meaningful consensus only if we agree on how the government's income can be increased or how its expenditure can be reduced.

What do you think as a citizen? Let's look at the revenue expenditure figures for 2003-04 and see if we can generate a consensus among ourselves. The aggregate revenue expenditure is 366227 crores. Of this, 76843 crores is "Plan" revenue expenditure. This is what is required as support for the Central Plan and Central assistance to States and UTs for their plans. So let's ignore this and assume this is desirable. We are now left with non-Plan revenue expenditure of 289384 crores. And we find that 123223 crores will be spent as interest payments on earlier government debt, repayment of principal and interest on earlier debt. What would you like to be done about interest payments? Would you suddenly like the government to announce that it will not honour its past debt obligations? This has indeed happened in other countries. But would you like that to happen in India? There will be a riot. By taking greater care about government expenditure (and revenue) in the future and by ensuring that the government borrows at market-determined rates of interest rather than interest rates that are artificially low, we can ensure that the government is discouraged from borrowing in the future. But what happens to the debt that has already been contracted?

Next we find 44347 crores being spent on defence. Notice that this is revenue expenditure on defence, not capital expenditure. Capital expenditure on defence is another 20953 crores. Anyone who questions defence expenditure will be accused of being a traitor. But do we need such huge expenditure on defence revenue expenditure? 49907 crores will be spent on subsidies. Mind you, this doesn't include all subsidies. It only includes subsidies that show up as subsidies in the Central government's account books, such as subsidies on food, fertilizer, LPG and PDS kerosene. 15466 crores will be spent on pensions.

Let's look at these figures slightly differently. Add 123223 crores of interest payments, 44347 crores of defence revenue expenditure, 49907 cores of subsidies and 15466 crores of pensions. That adds up to 232943 crores. Notice that combined revenue receipts add up to 253935 crores. That is, we have 20992 crores left for all the other things the government wants to do. In fact, if we add defence capital expenditure, we have virtually no money left. What do you expect Jaswant Singh to do? What do you expect any Finance Minister to do? The government is bankrupt. This state of affairs cannot go on indefinitely. To change matters, we need a consensus on what should be done about those major items of revenue expenditure – interest payments, defence, subsidies and pensions.

Quite often, people say that the government is not doing enough. Why focus on these to the exclusion of government employees? Government employees do nothing and are paid a lot, not to forget perks. Had it not been for the Fifth Central Pay Commission and its recommendations, life wouldn't have been so difficult. This argument is partly true and partly false. It is true that the government hasn't done much about downsizing government expenditure and 10 volumes of reports submitted by the Expenditure Reforms Commission are rotting in the dustbins. It is also true that payment to government employees bears no relation to their productivity and there is at least 10 per cent over-staffing (if not more) in any Ministry or government department you care to scrutinize. But do remember that for the Central government, the quantitative importance of salaries to Central government staff is not much. Pensions are a different matter. The signal is no doubt important.

The Central government employs 3.49 million people. Their salaries amount to 18740 crores, their allowances amount to 14298 crores and their travel allowances amount to 1305 crores. Certainly, these should be reduced. But the quantitative impact isn't going to be much.

25

Reforming Subsidies

EARLIER, I have referred to the bankruptcy that confronts the Central government (and State governments). The government needs to do certain things, such as in social and physical infrastructure. But until government expenditure is reformed, there simply isn't any money. And reforming government expenditure means resolving the problems of interest payments, defence expenditure, subsidies and pensions.

Take subsidies. Who can deny that the poor should have subsidies? Poverty is of course a relative concept. As development proceeds, the bar is raised. Poverty in the United States is not quite the same as poverty in India. Did you know that 72 per cent of those below the poverty line in the United States own one or more cars, 50 per cent have air conditioning, 72 per cent have washing machines, 20 per cent have dishwashers, 60 per cent have microwaves, 93 per cent have color television sets, 60 per cent have VCRs and 41 per cent own their own homes? Let's not talk about the US poverty line. Let's also not talk about the internationally used poverty line of 1 US dollar per day. In accordance with this, 34.7 per cent of the Indian population is estimated to be below the poverty line. (Actually, this is 1 US dollar per day in 1985 prices. In today's prices, it is more like 2 US dollars per day.) Let's talk instead of our own national poverty line. The NSS (National Sample Survey) collects data on expenditure and using these data, the Planning Commission computes poverty figures. NSS doesn't collect data with large enough samples every year. The last such large sample data go back to 1999-2000. There has been some controversy about the reliability of this survey, but let's ignore that also. We know that at an all-India level, 26 per cent of the Indian population was below the poverty line in 1999-2000. Strictly speaking, these BPL (below the poverty line) households should be entitled to subsidies. 26 per cent of the Indian population amounts to 260 million people. If you want to stretch things a bit and allow for increases in population, perhaps 300 million people.

The budget tells us that in 2003-04, Rs. 49,907 crores will be spent on subsidies. Notice that these are subsidies in accordance with the Central government's budgetary classifications, that is, subsidies on account of food, fertilizer, LPG and PDS kerosene. There are other subsidies that come out of State government budgets and these aren't included. Moreover, these are explicit subsidies. There are other subsidies that are not counted as subsidies, but are left implicit. If you include all subsidies, the way you should, I suspect the figure will be more like Rs. 60,000 crores a year.

Think of it in the following way. This is an argument I have already made. But it is important enough for it to be made again. And again and again. Let's give this Rs. 60,000 crores directly as cash transfers to those 260 million people. Work it out for yourself. Each poor person will get Rs. 2307 a year. If there are 6 people in each poor household, each poor household will get Rs. 13,842 a year. Do poor households really get the equivalent of this money? Had they really got the equivalent of this money, the face of poverty in India would have been quite different. In the late 1980s, the late Prime Minister, Rajiv Gandhi, made an off the cuff kind of remark. He said that, out of every one rupee that is spent in the name of the poor, not more than 15 per cent reaches the target beneficiary. This was an off the cuff kind of remark, not based on any research studies. But it has been quoted quite often. But subsequently, there has been research on success of anti-poverty programmes and these find that not more than 20 per cent of money spent actually reaches target beneficiaries. In some Planning Commission studies, the figure is found to be as low as 6 per cent. The truly poor benefit little. Instead, subsidies accrue to those who don't deserve them. They accrue to urban middle classes who don't deserve such subsidies. Think of monthly tuition fees in any under-graduate course in Delhi University. Less than a tube of toothpaste. Does this reflect the true value of education imparted? If not, there is a subsidy component and who benefits from this subsidy?

People sometimes think that the 80 per cent, 85 per cent or 94 per cent that is swallowed up, represents corruption. That's not quite true. There is indeed an element of corruption. But a significant amount is actually spent on running these anti-poverty programmes. Administrative costs are significant, given the long vertical chain or hierarchy in administering these programmes. Digressing a bit from subsidies, take the centrally sponsored schemes (CSSs) run by the government, usually in the social sectors. No one knows how many CSSs there are. There are at least 250. Some say there are more than 400. Sometimes the government doesn't even remember that such a specific CSS actually exists. Yet, we spend money on them. Part of the reason why no one knows is because earlier, the Centre gave money to States for specific programmes. These days, there are block transfers. We do know that in the 1980s, the share of CSSs in plan expenditure of Central government ministries was around 30 per cent. Today, the figure is around 70 per cent. The point is, do these CSSs benefit anyone at all?

Should the Central government at all decide what CSSs are worthwhile? Shouldn't it be left to local bodies to decide?

Shouldn't the money be passed downwards, not just to States, but further down below, so that the money is actually spent on what people want? This decentralization argument also extends to subsidies. Yes, there is a lot of unwarranted euphoria over *panchayat*s. Yes, *panchayat*s are also subject to corruption. But because the rungs in the hierarchy become less, less will be swallowed up in administrative costs. And if spliced with Right to Information Acts and access to information and combined with civil society pressure, as in Rajasthan, the efficiency of expenditure can also be ensured. Expenditure can be linked to actual improvement in outcomes.

Everyone in the country cannot be poor. Everyone in the country cannot expect subsidies. By all means, let us target subsidies towards BPL households. This targeting becomes easier if you decentralize downwards. One such successful identification exercise, driven by the community, is the Kudumbashree scheme run in Kerala. Forget the NSS. Instead, use easily measured criteria to identify the poor – poor quality of house, lack of access to safe drinking water, lack of access to sanitary latrines, number of illiterate adults in the family, single income households, number of individuals getting barely two meals a day or less, number of children below the age of five in the family, number of cases of alcoholism or drug addiction in the family and membership of socially disadvantaged groups (SCs/STs).

Targeting of subsidies is possible. But those who have unnecessarily obtained things free, don't want to let go.

26

Interest Rates
and Interest Payments

HAVING talked about subsidies, let's now turn our attention to interest payments. The government's interest burden depends on the principal and the interest rate. What should the country's interest rate be?

The answer depends on whether we have in mind the real interest rate or the nominal interest rate. The nominal interest rate is the interest rate as it stands. The real interest rate is the nominal interest rate minus the rate of inflation. Let's talk about the real rate of interest first.

Why should there be a positive real rate of interest? Let's ignore for the moment, the difference between a borrowing rate and a lending rate. If I save, I am cutting down on present consumption and am saving for the purposes of future consumption. The economic theory of interest rates is based on the argument that there should be a premium on future consumption. That's the reason the real rate of interest should be positive. Not all economists agree. There are indeed those who argue that there is nothing special about future consumption. Present consumption and future consumption should be treated in exactly the same way. Therefore, the real rate of interest should be zero. Even if I accept the argument about a positive real rate of interest, how much should that be? Looking around at developed countries, the figure that suggests itself is not more than 1 per cent. I could have argued that in a capital scarce country like India, the real rate of interest should be more than 1 per cent. But with globalization, and free cross-border movements of capital, this becomes a meaningless argument. Thus, the real rate of interest in India should also be not more than 1 per cent. Perhaps even 0 per cent.

To get the nominal rate of interest, we now need to figure out the rate of inflation. Inflation is defined as an increase in the price level. People don't always understand this nuance. The government says, the rate of inflation is declining. People say, we don't believe you – the price level isn't coming down. The rate of inflation declining simply means that the rate at which prices were increasing is coming down. For prices to actually decline, you would need the inflation rate to be negative. To come back to the inflation rate, there are all kinds of commodities (and services) in the world. Some show higher increases in prices. Others show lower increases in prices. Still others may actually show price declines. To obtain an idea of what is happening to the overall price level, one needs to aggregate across all these commodities and in this process of aggregation, each commodity will have a weight. This results in the creation of a price index. The behavior of the index naturally depends on the commodities that are included and their weights and these are also occasionally revised. Subject to this, in India we have a wholesale price index (WPI) and a consumer price index (CPI). More accurately, we have three different CPI series – the consumer price index for industrial workers (CPI-IW), the consumer price index for urban non-manual employees (CPI-UNME) and the consumer price index for agricultural labour (CPI-AL). Across these indices, the commodities included and their weights vary. Therefore, the behaviour of these indices also varies a little.

As consumers, we should react more to CPI behaviour. As producers, we should react more to WPI behaviour. Usually, when inflation figures in newspaper headlines, it is the WPI that people are talking about. This is because the WPI data come out faster. The CPI data are available with a time lag. Apart from that, the WPI that figures in newspaper headlines is what is known as point-to-point inflation. That is, it is inflation as compared to the price level prevailing exactly one year ago. This is not quite the same as what inflation is on an annual basis. On an annual basis, regardless of whether we use WPI or CPI, the inflation rate in India today is between 4 per cent and 5 per cent, closer actually to 4 per cent. But even if we accept 5 per cent, the nominal interest rate in India should be 6 per cent and no more. Quite logically, if you put your money in a fixed deposit in a bank today, you will be lucky if you get more than 5 per cent. To get higher returns, you must be prepared to take risk, such as in the equity market. The return then reflects a risk premium.

So far so good. But in India we have things known as small savings – National Savings Certificates (NSCs) or the Public Provident Fund (PPF). These are nothing but the government borrowing from citizens. At what rate does the government borrow? In 2001, a committee was set up under the Chairmanship of Dr. Y.V. Reddy, the present Governor of the RBI. This committee was supposed to examine the administered interest rate mechanism, such as interest rates offered on small savings. Remember that small savings are also linked to tax exemptions. The Reddy Committee found that if you take into account tax exemptions, the rate of return on small savings was between 17 per cent and 19 per cent. This is the rate at which the government borrowed. Should the government borrow at such rates, when inflation rates have dropped?

Several issues arise. First, should we expect such high rates of return when there is no risk? Thanks to instances like UTI, the government itself has of course convinced us that zero-risk high returns are possible. But if the government is going to offer such high rates of interest, banks will also have to offer high deposit rates to attract depositors. And because banks (or financial institutions) are not in the business of social service, lending rates will also be high. Most importantly, the genuinely poor don't have money to put in these small savings. But by offering such high returns on small savings, the government is depriving the poor, either through inflation or by not spending on things it should be spending on. In other words, high returns on small savings are a regressive transfer from the poor to the rich. The rich may want these. But the poor can't afford such transfers. The problem is, who listens to the poor?

Clearly, we need to reduce interest rates on government borrowings. This has indeed been done. And this reduces the future interest payment burden. What happens to the present interest rate burden? The government can't default. Some people say that privatization proceeds should be earmarked for retiring government debt. Because money is fungible, that is, money for one purpose can be freely converted into money for some other purpose, this argument is really important as a signal and no more. We need to reduce government expenditure and increase government income. There is no other solution.

27

Defence Expenditure and Pensions

WE have talked about other elements of current government expenditure. We still need to talk about defence expenditure and pensions. The problem with defence expenditure is that it is impossible to question this without being accused of being a traitor, especially when terrorism is a problem everywhere. But consider what we propose to spend on defence in 2003-04. Rs. 20,593 crores is capital expenditure and that can perhaps be left unquestioned. But Rs. 44,347 crores of defence expenditure is revenue expenditure. Today, defence expenditure is around 2.5 per cent of GDP. Perhaps it can't really be reduced. Perhaps it needs to be increased to 3 per cent of GDP. But as a country, we do need to ask the question, do we want defence expenditure or do we want education and health expenditure? Economics is all about trade-offs, about alternative uses for scarce resources, about opportunity costs. Many Economics text-books still depict this national choice in terms of a guns versus butter choice. For us, guns versus schools is perhaps more appropriate. That apart, given whatever strategic objectives we have, are those objectives best met when 68 per cent of defence expenditure is revenue expenditure? When significant amounts are spent on wages and pensions. Almost 11,000 crores are spent on defence pensions.

As I said earlier, 3.5 million people work for the Central government. Despite reforms and talk of downsizing, this number hasn't dropped at all. The only occasion when this number dropped a bit was in October 2000, when employees in the Department of Telecommunications began to be shown as employees of Bharat Sanchar Nigam Limited and therefore, ceased to be counted as Central government employees. Of the 3.5 million Central government employees, 1.5 million are in the Ministry of Railways alone. As a number, 3.5 million is not that large and savings from downsizing government (at least at the Central government level) aren't going to be significant. But it is extremely important as a signal. The problem is not so much with this figure of 3.5 million, but with what these people do. Do we need 42 Ministries? What precisely do the Ministries of Coal, Mines, Information & Broadcasting, Planning, Steel and Textiles do? Beyond Ministries, we have Departments. Why do we need a Department of Culture? If no other country in the world needs an official song and drama division, why do we need one? With Ministries, we have Ministers, Cabinet and State. Some with no charge whatsoever. We have Secretaries, lower-level civil service posts and Class III and IV support staff. What does a peon do, other than sit on a stool and switch the green light to red and the red one to green? In most instances, do we need anyone between the Section Officer and the Joint Secretary and between the Joint Secretary and the Secretary?

It is impossible to obtain a precise figure on what percentage of Central government staff is dysfunctional. A really conservative estimate will be 10 per cent. Several reports, including recommendations of the Fifth Central Pay Commission, talked about downsizing. There were 10 volumes of reports brought out by the Expenditure Reforms Commission. Budget speeches talked about downsizing. We were told surplus staff would be identified. They would be transferred to a surplus pool and retrained. If retraining wasn't possible, they would be subjected to voluntary retirement schemes (VRS). Nothing has happened. You must have noticed that budget speeches now have an action taken report (ATR). The ATR tells you what has happened to promises made in earlier budgets. If you notice, the 2003-04 budget speech and the related ATR has dropped all reference to recommendations of the Expenditure Reforms Commission. No downsizing is possible and nothing will get done. Instead the LTC (leave travel concession) for government employees will be withdrawn and then re-introduced. At best, we will have a freeze on new recruitment, although that provision can also be circumvented. Since roughly 2 per cent government employees retire every year, at the end of 5 years we will eliminate 10 per cent. If we are lucky. Every government car costs at least Rs. 15,000 per month to run, including the driver's salary and cost of petrol. For Rs. 15,000 a month, we can easily run 4 schools in villages every year. Think about it.

But as I said earlier, at the Central government level, the quantitative importance of downsizing number of government employees isn't that much. Except for the pension angle. Recruitment of government employees isn't spread out evenly over time. Recruitments are often bunched together and these people, who were recruited at more or less the same time, will also retire at roughly the same time. This is already beginning to assume serious proportions, both for civil and defence staff and will become an even more serious problem in the next 10 years. Forget State governments for the moment. But this is also going to kill the Central government. Don't misunderstand. For people who are already in government service, or those who were in government service and have retired, no one is talking about changing their pension terms. That would amount to breach of contract, so to speak. But surely, for new government staff, there is some other mechanism we can visualize.

Once I retire, I need an assured income stream per month. I can get a gratuity or money from a provident fund (PF), PF being nothing other than a gratuity. The problem with the present system of course is that there are 20 different reasons under which I can withdraw money from the PF. Meanwhile, because PF deductions are tax exempt, there is an incentive for me to put the money in. Having availed of the tax exemption, there is an incentive for me to take the money out. Therefore, at the time of retirement, I don't have the money I am supposed to have. Of course, I can divide the PF amount into an employer and an employee contribution, but the argument isn't affected. Assuming I have the PF or gratuity money, surely it is my business to decide where I am going to invest it so as to enable flow of that steady income stream per month. Why should that be anyone else's business?

What we have now, in addition to the PF, is a pension scheme. Notice the pension I get doesn't depend on what I have put in as my contribution. Notice I have no flexibility in deciding where the corpus that gets me my pension will be invested. The pension I get has no relationship with the returns the pension fund is generating. All this is plain illogical and needs to change for future entrants into government service.

28

State Budgets

So far, I have used numbers from the Central budget. But the problem is even more serious for State budgets. Constitutionally, primary education, primary health care and law and order are mostly State subjects. If we come along and say the government must spend 6 per cent of GDP on education or health, that expenditure will primarily have to be routed through State governments.

In 2002, the Planning Commission brought out the *National Human Development Report*. This has figures from State budgets for the year 1998-99. Yes, these figures are old. But the issues haven't changed. Since these are figures for State governments, we should of course consider State domestic product (SDP) rather than GDP (gross domestic product). Using these figures, let's ask a question. Which States spent more than 5 per cent of SDP on education? The answer is Arunachal Pradesh, Assam, Himachal Pradesh, Jammu & Kashmir, Manipur, Meghalaya, Sikkim and Tripura. The major States don't figure in this list. Which States spent more than 5 per cent of SDP on health? Not a single one. The highest expenditure was in Sikkim and this was 4.92 per cent of SDP. And remember, these figures are only about expenditure. They tell us nothing about the efficiency of this expenditure.

Everyone agrees the government must spend on capital expenditure. Not on the revenue account. Let's then ask a different question. Which States spent more than 20 per cent of expenditure on capital expenditure? The answer is Arunachal Pradesh, Manipur, Mizoram and Delhi. Clearly, life is not as it should be. Fiscal and revenue deficits don't allow the government from spending where it should be spending. In 1993-94, the combined State fiscal deficit was 2.35 per cent of GDP. In 1999-2000, it increased to 4.71 per cent of GDP. In 1993-94, the combined State revenue deficit was 0.45 per cent of GDP. In 1999-2000, this increased to 2.96 per cent of GDP. Today, it is difficult to be believe that in 1990-91, many States had revenue surpluses. Today, it is difficult to find a State where the revenue deficit is less than 7 per cent of SDP. Therefore, the position has deteriorated in the 1990s. Deficits have increased, State debt has increased. Borrow more to repay old debt. On top of that, State governments have offered all kinds of guarantees. Naturally, the government can't perform its core functions.

There is no great disagreement about why the deterioration took place. Here are some of the reasons.

(1) There was the Fifth Central Pay Commission to determine salaries and pensions of Central government staff. The Pay Commission made several recommendations about downsizing also. No one listened to those. Instead, salaries and pensions increased. Logically, there was no requirement that these recommendations should also be accepted by State governments. But politically, that is difficult to do. In the Central government, the hikes applied to Ministries and Departments. At the State government level, they also applied to aided institutions and local bodies. The net result is that, depending on the State, between two-thirds and three-fourths of revenue goes on salaries and pensions. Where is the money for

anything else? Naturally, developmental expenditure gets affected.

(2)   There was a downturn in the economy from around 1998, especially in manufacturing. This affected Central tax revenue collections and correspondingly, State share of this revenue. The downturn also adversely affected sales tax collected by States. While this downturn argument is true, we must also recognize that States introduced several sales tax-related incentives to attract investments to the respective States and this also affected State-level revenue collection. In fact, the reduction in sales tax revenue collected by States actually preceded the downturn.

(3)   Other than tax revenue, States can obtain revenue from public sector undertakings (PSUs). There are almost 1000 PSUs at State government level. At least 75,000 crores of rupees have been invested in statutory corporations. At least 42,000 crores of rupees have been invested in government-owned companies. Both as equity and loans. The returns obtained are anyone's guess, because several State-level PSUs have not finalized their accounts for several years. At least 200 State-level PSUs don't have up-to-date accounts. For accounts that exist for State-level PSUs, we find the actual return is around 0 per cent. Under the Electricity (Supply) Act of 1948, State Electricity Boards (SEBs) were supposed to get an annual return of 3 per cent. In 1998-99, the actual return was minus 18.7 per cent. The road transport undertakings are no better. But no State government wants to touch these.

(4)   Related to PSUs is the subsidy problem. The government offers several services. Some of these are known as social services. Others are known as economic services, such as irrigation, power or roads. No one will

object to the genuinely poor obtaining subsidies and being charged less than the actual cost of producing these services. But surely, everyone in the country cannot be poor. Courtesy populism, however, these subsidies have increased. Let's take two examples. In 1990-91, State governments recovered 1.17 per cent of the expenditure on education through fees. In 1998-99, this figure declined to 0.85 per cent. In 1990-91, State governments recovered 37.05 per cent of the expenditure on electricity through charges. In 1998-99, the figure dropped to 11.84 per cent. Yet, fear of losing elections prevents State governments from imposing right user charges for services and targeting subsidies to those who are actually poor.

I don't understand how the poor benefit from this system. There is a difference between doing things for the poor and doing things in the name of the poor. Let's agree that the government's core functions are education, health, some forms of physical infrastructure and preserving law and order. I think we can also agree that these are the things that any "socialist" government should also be doing. However, to ensure that these core governance functions are delivered, the present system needs to change. Government expenditure and revenue have to be reformed, not just at the Central government level, but also at the State-government level, where the delivery of these core functions is often Constitutionally located. In fact, delivery is sometimes located lower down, at the local government level and we need to discuss revenue and expenditure for local governments also, urban local bodies (ULBs) and *panchayati raj* institutions (PRIs). We need to discuss decentralization. We need to talk about accountability and transparency of government expenditure, through Right to Information Acts. It's only then that we can argue that India has become a socialist country.

29

Public Sector Undertakings (PSUs)

WE have talked about the terrible shape Central and State government budgets are in. Without reforming public sector undertakings (PSUs), we can't solve the government's budgetary problem. This has both a revenue and an expenditure side. PSUs are supposed to bring in revenue, but they don't. On the other hand, losses suffered by PSUs require government expenditure in the form of subsidies. There are around 240 PSUs at the Central government level, around 1000 at the State level. Of course, there are different types of PSUs. Some are directly run by the government. Others have been set up as autonomous and independent companies. Still others, like the post office, railways or telecom (once upon a time) are run as departmental undertakings. Watches, bread, cycles and scooters are produced, or were produced, by PSUs. Services like banking, insurance, electricity and road transport are also provided by PSUs.

We have already agreed that the government's primary responsibility is education, health, some physical infrastructure and law and order. Why should the government ignore these core responsibilities and get into PSUs? In the late 1940s and early 1950s, many reasons were cited for the government to get into other areas through PSUs. PSUs were regarded as essential to ensuring development in India.

There are indeed situations where the market doesn't provide a good or a service. Economists refer to these as market failure. Market failure was the main reason why these temples of modern India were set up. Heavy industry had to be set up. How was the private sector going to set it up? It didn't have the capital market, the capital market wasn't sufficiently developed. It didn't have the technology. On the other hand, scarcity of foreign exchange meant that these things couldn't be imported.

Most ideas of market failure can be expressed through externalities. If my action has an effect on your life, that's an externality. Externalities can be positive, as well as negative. If I keep a dog and that keeps thieves away from your house also, you being my neighbour, that is a positive externality. But if my dog dirties up your garden, that's a negative externality. Externalities often don't have a market and market-determined prices. In the case of a positive externality, I can't charge you for part of my dog's food costs. And you can't charge me for cleaning up your garden. Private calculations are on the basis of marginal private cost and marginal private benefit. But society's calculations should be based on marginal social cost and marginal social benefit. If there are positive externalities, the marginal social benefit may be greater than the marginal private benefit. If there are negative externalities, the marginal social cost may be greater than the marginal private cost. In the case of protecting the environment, because there are negative externalities, we ask for government action. Similarly, there were areas where we wanted investments to take place because there were positive externalities. But private investments would be based on marginal private benefit, not marginal social benefit which was higher, and many investments wouldn't take place, even though they were desirable. This was the general idea behind the argument that PSUs should be set up. Fair enough. But we should ask a simple question. How many of these market failure kind of arguments are valid today?

There was also a different of argument behind setting up PSUs. That was linked to notions of equity and reducing inequality. The hypothesis is that the private sector leads to increased income differences and we have talked about socialism earlier. The private sector will lead to higher prices, for both goods and services. Think about it. If there are high prices and high profits are to be made, why shouldn't competition eliminate these high prices and high profits? The only possible answer is licensing, created by the government, and which generally used to be prevalent before 1991. In other words, the culprit behind high prices and high profits is licensing, not the private sector. Certainly it is not the case that there is pure and unadulterated competition if we simply remove licensing. We know that there are unfair and restrictive business practices that kill competition, or prevent it. That's the reason we need competition policy instruments, directed not only against unfair and restrictive business practices of the private sector, but also of the public sector. Notice also that if there are high prices and the truly poor suffer, we can always have a system of targeted subsidies for the truly poor. No need to set up PSUs for that purpose.

Some other arguments also crop up sometimes. We need PSUs to ensure balanced regional development. Once upon a time, the theory of economic development used to be full of discussions about balanced and unbalanced development. Sure, every region must develop. Sure, every country must develop. Every country has comparative advantages that it seeks to exploit. And every region also has comparative advantages that it should seek to exploit. That provides the source for growth. Balanced growth should not mean that I set up PSUs to produce steel in a region where there is no coal or iron ore. In the history of setting up PSUs in India, there are countless examples of such illogical decisions.

Yet another fallacious argument is about employment. PSUs are needed to generate employment. I have already mentioned the 240 Central PSUs. Many of these used to be in the private sector earlier. Life and death, entry and exit are inevitable. But because we didn't want sick private sector units to exit, they were absorbed into the public sector. Through nationalization. We are always bothered about protecting present employment, not ensuring future employment. Think of it in the following way. 6 million people work for PSUs, 394 million people work for the private sector. The inefficiency of PSUs also impacts the working of the private sector. If efficiency improves, GDP growth should go up. If we grow at 6 per cent a year, we will create 9 million new jobs a year. If we grow at 7.5 per cent a year, we will create 11 million jobs a year. In three years, we will recoup the entire present employment in PSUs. There are other and better ways of ensuring employment than creating PSUs.

30

Reforming PSUs

PSUs have often been described as temples of modern India. The nature of the temple is defined by the idol enshrined in the temple. And PSUs have never had Lakshmi, the goddess of wealth, instated in them. The Industrial Policy Resolutions of 1948 and 1956 didn't only expect PSUs to generate employment. They were also expected to generate surpluses. If prices are administered and there are monopolies, indicators of profit don't mean much. It is true that profitability in PSUs has increased a bit in the last ten years. At least for the Central PSUs. The rate of profit is around 5 per cent. If you have some money to invest, will you be satisfied with a rate of return of 5 per cent? Probably not. Because you can get much higher returns elsewhere. Economists refer to this idea as opportunity cost, the return these resources would have fetched elsewhere. Clearly, we shouldn't be satisfied with a rate of return of 5 per cent.

Besides, 5 per cent is an average. More than 120 of the 240 Central PSUs make losses. If you have bought the shares in a company, as a shareholder won't you be concerned if that company makes losses? After buying shares, you are part owner of that company. All of India's citizens are part owners of PSUs. Yet we don't seem to be bothered that PSUs don't give us dividends. We don't seem to be bothered that we have to pay for

the losses that PSUs make. For the 120 loss making Central PSUs, each Indian citizen has to pay the equivalent of 80 rupees a year. The poor also pay for these losses. If not through inflation and indirect taxes, through the opportunity costs of infrastructure that isn't built. Think of it in this way. Each PSU driver is paid at least Rs. 72.000 a year. With Rs. 72,000 a year, I can run three schools in villages.

If one looks at State-level PSUs, the situation is worse. More than 75 per cent of these haven't finalized their accounts for years on end. We don't even know what they are doing. Nor are we bothered. No one is going to object if PSUs remain and function on the basis of commercial principles. But that's not what they are doing. Those PSUs that aren't functioning properly should clearly exit. This point should be beyond debate.

Those who oppose PSU privatization may agree on this. But they will say, let us restructure PSUs first. Why must we sell them off immediately? Let's try to restructure them. Let's make them function according to commercial principles. If that fails, we will sell them off then. This is the kind of argument one heard in the 1980s and attempts were made to reform PSUs through memoranda of understanding (MOUs). That didn't work. Nor will any such restructuring idea work now. The problem lies in several of our laws, including the Constitution. Let me give you some examples.

Article 12 of the Constitution defines the State as follows. "In this Part, unless the context otherwise requires, the State includes the Government and Parliament of India and the Government and the Legislature of each of the States and all local or other authorities within the territory of India or under the control of the Government of India." The Constitution imposes certain social obligations on the State. Notice that thanks to the "under the control" expression, all PSUs become defined as State and accordingly, social obligations are imposed on them. This is regardless of whether government equity in the PSU is more or less than 50 per cent. As long as we have this, how can be ask PSUs to function on commercial principles? Under the Constitution, writ petitions can be brought against PSUs, Article 32 for the Supreme Court and Article 226 for High Courts. It is up to Parliament to scrutinize whether the State is performing its Constitutional obligation properly or not. So PSUs come under the purview of Parliament. There will be CAG audits, there will be misuse by the administrative Ministry concerned. For selecting senior management, there will be the Public Enterprise Selection Board (PESB). Other than the PESB, there will be the Department of Personnel, the Home Ministry, sometimes even the PMO. Subject to the Board, the CEO of a company has the right to take decisions. Which CEO of which PSU will have such a right? I should also mention Article 311 of the Constitution. Although not directly relevant to PSUs, this does apply to all civil service posts. Thanks to Article 311, it is almost impossible to sack anyone.

Then there is *the Prevention of Corruption Act*, passed in 1988. Everyone wants corruption to go. No problems with that. But Section 13(1)d(iii) of *the Prevention of Corruption Act* states, "A public servant is said to commit the offence of criminal misconduct if he while holding office as a public servant, obtains for any person any valuable thing or pecuniary advantage without any public interest." Any decision you take will benefit a third party. We are not talking about the public servant taking a bribe for his or her benefit. If any decision benefits a third party, and it is impossible to prove that this benefit to the third party is in the public interest, which public servant will take decisions?

Threatened with the CBI and vigilance enquiries, every public servant will become risk averse and refuse to take decisions. How do you get PSUs to function according to commercial principles? Therefore, given this thicket of laws, the idea of restructuring PSUs remains a hypothetical one. And the experiment won't work, as it didn't in the 1980s.

We should therefore sell PSUs. Some people will object, saying that PSUs serve a strategic purpose. We shouldn't sell PSUs in the strategic sector. The trouble is, what is strategic and what is not? Barring arms, ammunition, defence equipment, atomic energy, radioactive minerals and some part of railways, I can't think of anything else that should be strategic. Certainly not petrol pumps. There can indeed be a debate about the best method to sell PSUs. Notice that to get out of the thicket of controls, one has to reduce government equity to below 50 per cent, although sometimes, even that will not do. The answer about the best mode of privatization varies from case to case. In general, sales of minority stakes through limited public offerings are more transparent and dissipate the political resistance, but also bring reduced values, compared to strategic sales to a strategic partner. Almost tautologically, strategic sales can't be that transparent. There will be disputes about valuation, about whether we value the PSU as a functioning entity or one that is being completely wound up. But privatization, at the Centre and in the States, has to take place.

31

Efficient Use of Capital

ANY economist will tell you that output can be increased in two ways. First, increase the amount of inputs that go into production, examples of inputs being land, labour, capital and entrepreneurship. This is known as the extensive method for increasing output. Second, improve the efficiency with which existing inputs are being used in the production process. This is known as the intensive method. I have tried to argue that we have emphasized increasing the use of capital, by trying to step up saving and investment rates. In contrast, we haven't paid enough attention to improving the efficiency with which capital is used. PSUs are but one example of this. Competition requires free entry and exit. If exit doesn't occur, capital is stuck in an old enterprise, although it has better uses elsewhere. I have already mentioned sick private sector units that weren't allowed to close down, but were nationalized using *the Industries (Development and Regulation) Act* of 1951.

The lack of an exit policy characterized not only PSUs or private sector units that had been converted into PSUs, but also existing private sector ones. Unfortunately, exit policy in India has been equated with an exit policy for labour. That's not the case. When an enterprise is in trouble, management exits first. Then ownership exits. Finally, if necessary, labour exits.

Not all sick enterprises have obtained loans from scheduled commercial banks. For those that have, we have some data from RBI and we known that in March 2001, there were 252,947 sick enterprises. 249,630 belonged to the small-scale industry (SSI) category. Of the 3,317 sick enterprises that weren't SSI, 2942 were in the private sector, 255 were in the public sector, 106 were in the joint sector and 14 were cooperative units. 25,775 cores of bank loans were stuck in these sick units. This is just from banks. If one includes financial institutions, the figure will be higher. Non-performing assets (NPAs) of banks and financial institutions may be as high as 100,000 crores. Naturally, not all of this is backed with collateral. But certainly, collateral worth at least Rs. 40,000 crores is stuck. This 40,000 crores could have been used elsewhere.

One needn't discuss the reasons why an exit policy failed to evolve historically. Stated simply, *the Sick Industrial Companies (Special Provisions) Act* of 1985 didn't work properly. Nor did the Board for Industrial and Financial Reconstruction (BIFR), formed in 1987. There were problems with the definition of sickness. There was too much of court intervention. A lot of resources were frittered away in trying to rehabilitate sick companies that could never be rehabilitated. Talking of court intervention, let me give you a quote from Section 69 of *the Transfer of Property Act* of 1882. This governed situations where a mortgage could be foreclosed and the collateral used, without court intervention. Until recently, this section said, "A mortgagee, or any person acting on his behalf, shall, subject to the provisions of this section, have power to sell or concur in selling the mortgaged property or any part thereof, in default of payment of the mortgage-money, without the intervention of the Court in the following cases and in no others, namely: (a) where the mortgage is an English mortgage, and neither the mortgagor nor the mortgagee is a Hindu, Muhammadan or Buddhist." What is odd is that this 1882 language continued till 2002.

There is now a new law known as *the Securitisation, Reconstruction of Financial Assets and Enforcement of Security Interest Act*. This will make exit easier and a market for securitisation of financial assets will gradually be built up. But this doesn't solve the exit problem entirely. A sick enterprise may have obtained credit without securities. It may have financed itself through equity. So there are issues connected with revamping *the Companies Act* of 1956. We must exit from this maze of BIFR, the Company Law Board and High Courts. Exit is an inevitable part of competition. It is natural, as natural as entry is. Exit must be facilitated. This is an issue not just for limited liability companies, but all enterprises. There is a serious exit problem for the SSI sector, a problem that often receives inadequate attention.

We don't have satisfactory bankruptcy or personal insolvency laws. I am simplifying somewhat, but what happens is something like the following. If I am in the SSI sector, I have pledged my house or my wife's jewellery to obtain loans from a bank or financial institution. When the enterprise is in trouble and goes sick, I default on electricity charges. I default on sales taxes. I default on provident fund payments. All the relevant laws state that these defaults will be treated as equivalent to default on land revenue. Land revenue laws were passed by the British, often in the 1870s. All land laws state that default of land revenue is a criminal offence. Accordingly, countless entrepreneurs are picked up and dumped in jail. Dumping entrepreneurs in jails helps them commit suicide, it doesn't help in recovering dues. Fresh entrepreneurship is required to get back the dues. Because fresh entrepreneurship is killed, we discourage all entrepreneurship. We punish entrepreneurship.

Since the issue of capital has come up, let me also mention Hernando de Soto. Hernando de Soto wrote two influential books. The first one, titled "The Other Path" was published in 1989. The second one, titled "The Mystery of Capital" was published in 2000. I have mentioned "The Other Path" earlier. "The Mystery of Capital" argues that the main difference between developed and developing countries is that in developing countries we deprive the poor of the most important resource they have, namely, land. This is the only form of capital the poor really have. Because we prevent land markets from developing, because we have no clear land rights and land titles, there are no land markets. In India, we have prevented land markets from developing, not only through outmoded and dysfunctional land ceiling legislation, but also by often declaring tenancy illegal. That merely drives tenancy underground. There is no incentive to invest in land. As for land titles, cadastral surveys are used to determine land titles. Did you know that the last cadastral surveys were done in India by the British in the 1920s? There have been no cadastral surveys after that. To use Hernando de Soto's language, land remains "dead capital" in India. In England, the Enclosure Movement paved the way for the Industrial Revolution. We haven't had that yet.

32

Efficient Use of Labour

OTHER than capital, labour is another input used in the production process. The 2001 Census tells us that India's population is 1.029 billion. The figure will be more now. From 1991 to 2001, that is, during the decade of the 1990s, the Indian population grew at an annual average rate of 2.134 per cent. Several people say that a high rate of growth of population is our biggest problem. Had the rate of population growth been lower, we would probably have become a developed country by now. Apparently, that does seem to be true. India's per capita income is 500 US dollars and we get per capita income by dividing total income with total population. So if India's population becomes half of what it is now, the per capita income will go up to 1000 dollars. If we can only eliminate half of our population, perhaps by murdering them, our developmental problems will be solved.

There is an obvious fallacy in this argument. We assume that this surplus or excess population is unproductive. So even if we eliminate them, the country's national income will be unchanged. We think of 1 billion mouths to feed. Not the 2 billion hands that go along with these 1 billion mouths. The billionth Indian was named Astha Arora. The word "Astha" can loosely be translated as belief. The parents had some faith in their daughter when they gave her that name. We have no faith in our population. But population is not only a liability. It is also an asset. Unfortunately, we convert all our assets into liabilities.

Age Structure

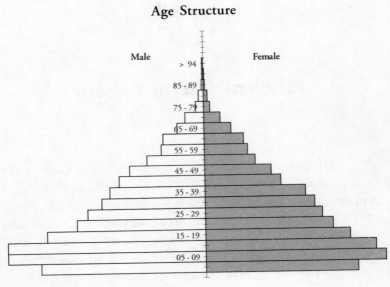

Source: NSSO, 1998-99

The labour force is not the same as total population. Those who are below 15 are not supposed to work. Nor are those who are over 60. The productive age-group is therefore defined as that which is between 15 and 59 years of age. 56.1 per cent of India's population is in this age-group. 56.1 per cent of 1.029 billion is 576 million. 576 million people who can actually be productive. That doesn't mean that all of this 576 million wants to work. The population that is actually in the labour force is probably around 410 million. Note that those who are babies today, will become adults in the future. That's the reason India's dependency ratio is declining and will decline even more in the future. Today, the dependency ratio is around 43.7 per cent. Around 2007, the population in the productive age-groups will increase from the present 56.1 per cent to around 62.3 per cent. Around 2012, it will increase to around 63.2 per cent.

The reason for the drop in the dependency ratio is easy to understand. The annual rate of growth in population was 2.134 per cent from 1991 to 2001. But that's not the rate of growth in population today. Today, the rate of population growth is probably around 1.8 or 1.9 per cent and in the next 10 years, will drop to around 1.5 per cent. Of course, there are inter-regional cum inter-State variations in this drop. The 1981 Census showed us that population rates of growth dropped in Kerala. The 1991 Census extended the lesson to Tamil Nadu. The 2001 Census extended the lesson to Andhra Pradesh. Indeed, rates of growth are still high in North India. But overall, fewer babies are being born today. That contributes partly to the drop in the dependency ratio. But babies who were born 20 or 25 years ago are entering the labour force now. That also contributes to the drop in the dependency ratio. So even though the rate of population growth slows to 1.5 per cent, the rate of growth in the labour force will continue to be around 2.5 per cent. India is going through a process of demographic transition. That helped GDP growth in South-East Asia and East Asia. Why should India be different?

When we say population is a problem, we often mean that public services can't be delivered properly. And these services, like education or health, are still largely provided by the public sector. The limited privatization is restricted to urban areas. Alternatively, we can't provide physical infrastructure like electricity, roads, sewage, drinking water and sanitation. The problem then lies with inefficient and inadequate delivery of these services. Why blame it on population?

Sometimes, we think we won't be able to feed this additional population. Every since the days of Malthus, we have feared that population growth will outstrip growth in food production. Take any agricultural product you want and compared the yields in India today with global yields. You don't even have to compare it with global yields. Compare it with the best yields achieved by developing countries. If agricultural productivity can be increased, and we don't even have to touch the best levels in the world, we will be able to feed double the population without any problems whatsoever. Remember that compared with many other countries, India has a much higher percentage of arable land. True, we have messed up our agricultural policies. But why blame it on population? True, we have messed up our urban planning. But why blame that on population? True, reforms haven't taken place in the rural sector. There are no employment opportunities there and migration pushes people into urban areas in search of jobs. But why blame that on population?

However, in addition to overall economic policies, three special points need to be made about efficient use of labour. First, there is an issue of unnecessarily rigid labour laws. This doesn't only mean *the Industrial Disputes Act* and its Chapter V-B, which make it impossible for retrenchment, layoff or closure to take place without the permission of the government. It also means the plethora of administrative law type regulations that make labour markets in the organized sector unnecessarily rigid. This encourages use of too much capital and too little labour. Second, employment requires growth. Without growth, how will we get employment? The composition of growth is also important, such as growth in the rural sector, with rural sector reforms required to ensure employment generation. Incidentally, employment growth has not grown as fast in the 1990s. Third, there is a regional angle also. Growth must occur where the surplus labour is located, in a geographical sense.

I have used the expression organized sector, so let me clarify what that means. There are three definitions of organized and unorganized, although all three lead to the same kind of identification. First, under *the Factories Act*, if you employ 10 or more workers and use power or employ 20 or more workers and don't use power, you are in the organized sector. Second, there is a specific definition of small-scale industry (SSI), expressed in terms of a threshold level of investment in plant and machinery. Third, there is a turnover limit, below which, I don't have to pay excise. Whichever version of organized is used, around 8 per cent of the Indian labour force is employed in the organized sector.

33

School Education and the State's Role

EFFICIENT usage of labour requires education and skills. We have also agreed that the State has a role to play in education. Of course, education means different things. There is school education. There is vocational education. There is higher education. The nature of State intervention can, and should, vary. Perhaps one should acknowledge that India's educational indicators have improved in the 1990s. As per the Census, the literacy rate has increased from 52 per cent in 1991 to 65 per cent in 2001. Certainly, there are problems with the Census definition of literacy. But this is a constant problem. Notwithstanding this problem, the improvement has occurred. Among major States, the problem is really in undivided Bihar and UP. These are the only States where the literacy rate is lower than 60 per cent. Literacy has crossed 60 per cent even in a State like Rajasthan. This doesn't of course mean that we ignore gender disparities or differential access for SCs or STs.

There is an adult illiteracy problem and there is a role for schemes directed towards ensuring adult literacy. But this adult literacy problem will disappear over time, if the problem of children's access to education can be addressed. Then, a literacy

Education - Continued Progress in Literacy

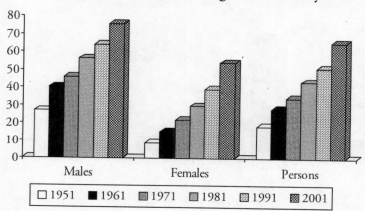

Source: Census of India

Primary Gross Enrollment Rate

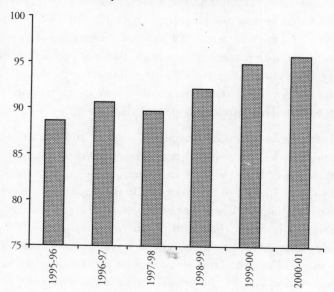

Source: Selected Educational Statistics 2000-2001

Primary School Drop-Out Rates

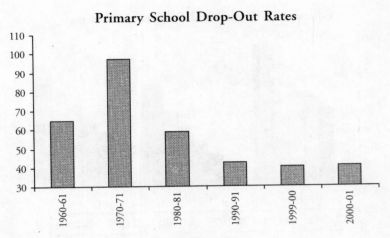

Source: Selected Educational Statistics 2000-2001

rate of 90 per cent is not a distant dream. Are children getting enrolled in schools? This can be gauged through the gross enrolment rate (GER). The GER for children aged between 6 and 11 years is now 96 per cent. The GER for children aged between 11 and 14 years is 59 per cent. There are differences across States, differences across gender. But it is probably correct to say that enrolment is becoming less of a problem. The problem is one of ensuring that children stay in school once they are enrolled. The problem is one of drop-outs.

India is a large and heterogeneous country and one can't have the same model everywhere, regardless of town or village. After all, there are 550,000 villages in India. Can we expect the same ideas to work in all 550,000 villages? By the way, why do we have so many villages? There are villages where the number of inhabitants is fewer than 200. If there are so many villages, ensuring that there is a school within 1 kilometre of each village is an impossible task. This is also true of providing other public services. Quite clearly, the private sector is not going to go and set up schools in remote villages. That has to remain a State function. But is it essential to have a school within 1 kilometre of your habitation? Provided roads and transport infrastructure exist, 5, 10 or even 15 kilometres should be no problem at all. Provided that the schools provided good quality education. I suspect that if roads and transport infrastructure improve, many of these 550,000 villages will disappear. They exist today, because I have no means of traveling 5 kilometres to earn my livelihood. I have no idea how many villages will remain if this improvement in physical infrastructure takes place. But providing public services should be less of a problem.

Competition is good for everything and the principle is no different for education. If private sector alternatives exist to government schools, that competition is good for students and parents and competition also improves quality of education imparted by government schools. This idea of competition may not be possible in every village. But it is certainly possible in urban areas, slums and even larger villages. Quite often, it is argued that private sector education will be expensive. It will prevent access to poor households. Not quite true. James Tooley has done some work in what he calls private budget schools in the slums of Hyderabad. We find that the tuition fees are more or less the same in government schools and private budget schools, because private budget schools have lower administrative costs. Administrative costs can be 65 per cent in government schools, but 30 per cent in private budget schools. Private budget schools also offer scholarships for the poor. Remember also that provided good quality education is available, studies show that even poor households are prepared to pay higher fees. They refuse to pay higher fees because quality of education imparted in government schools is poor.

That apart, if we are interested in subsidizing school education for the poor, what is to prevent us from directly offering scholarships or other forms of subsidies to targeted BPL households? No one will object. No one will object if BPL households get free uniforms, free text-books, mid-day meals and health services in schools. No one will object if there is a voucher system that subsidizes school education and allows the student to take the voucher to whichever school he or she wants, provided that such competition is possible. The objection is to the present system of government expenditure on schooling. We have government school teachers who don't teach. Giving them 10 increments each increases government expenditure on education. But that doesn't automatically improve educational outcomes. In State after State, more than 95 per cent of expenditure on school education is on salaries and pensions of teachers. No money left for school infrastructure, text-books or blackboards.

The government-delivered educational system has no flexibility. I think the reason educational indicators have improved in India in the 1990s is partly due to increased NGO (non-government organization) involvement. This has also increased awareness about returns from education. In some cases, NGOs have run schools, often through public-private partnerships (PPPs). The PPPs can also involve handing over public sector assets to private sector management, government school infrastructure being a case in point. There is also an issue of deciding what we mean by government. Is it a centralized government or has decision-making been decentralized? There have been such successful experiments involving parent-teacher associations (PTAs) or *panchayat*s. Decentralization increases accountability and takes providers closer to users of services.

There are 8.5 lakh schools in India, although some people say the actual figure is closer to 10 lakh. One doesn't expect the same model to work everywhere. But the success of the 1990s indicates the directions for reform – choice, accountability, decentralization, transparency. Finally, I think I should mention that licensing is not dead in India. You may think it is dead. But it is only dead for manufacturing. For something like schools, it is still very much around. Look at *the Delhi Education Act* of 1973 and the associated rules. All States have similar laws. Why can't we completely free up choice? Let schools decide which Boards they want to affiliate themselves to. Let there be choice in determining syllabi and methods of examination. Let us finally end this learning by rote system, devised by the British to generate clerks who aren't supposed to think. As for standardized testing by an external agency, that will eventually happen. Like the Scholastic Aptitude Test (SAT) in the United States.

34

Higher Education

UNLIKE school education, I think the scope or need for State intervention in higher education is limited. But before higher education, let me quickly mention vocational education. What utter garbage floats around in the name of vocational education. Every boy has to a carpenter. Every girl has to be a tailor. With competition and choice, I think vocational education will take care of itself and need not exist as a separate category. A proper apprentice system will evolve.

The WTO (World Trade Organization) has some agreements on opening up service sectors. The Doha Development Agenda (DDA) negotiations are going on, as part of the WTO's negotiating process. Until these negotiations are finalized and commitments materialize, the Uruguay Round's (1986-94) commitments remain applicable. Under the Uruguay Round agreements, India has no compulsion to open up higher education to foreign entry. But this may very well happen under the DDA. Though not immediately. Alarm bells are already ringing, as if disaster will strike us if that happens. Competition is good for everything else. But not for higher education.

Why should there be disaster? I read in a magazine that per capita, India produces the most number of Ph.Ds in the world.

Not absolute numbers, but per capita. I find this difficult to believe and the magazine had no source, so I have no means of checking. But regardless of this figure, everyone seems to think that India has enormous strengths in education. There are 7926 general colleges, 2223 professional colleges, 254 universities, deemed universities and institutions of national importance. These are figures for 2000-01. Compared to 1999-2000, we added 223 new colleges and 18 new universities. Why should we be scared of competition?

Increase in Number of Colleges

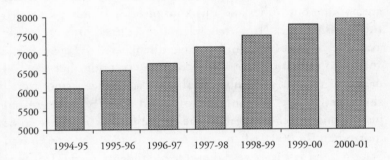

Source: Selected Educational Statistics, 2001-02

There seems to be a problem with obtaining precise figures on higher education. But let's juggle around a bit with figures, for what they are worth. Across all streams, how many students do you think a college can handle? 1000 should be fine and 10,149 colleges (7926 + 2223) should then be able to handle 10,149,000 students. How many students should a university be able to handle? Depends on the type of university, but on an average, 5000 should be manageable. Even if I ignore some deemed universities and institutions of national importance as smaller entities and assume the number of proper universities as 238, that's still 1,190,000 students. 10,149,000 plus 1,190,000 is 11,339,000 and that falls short of 7,730,800 students enrolled in institutions of higher education. UGC or AICTE may choose to correct the precise figures I have cited. But I think the broad orders of magnitude are correct. *Ipso facto*, there is no shortage of seats for higher education and remember, we are adding new colleges and universities every year.

Try telling that to parents and students. Okay, we may have problems with CBSE (or State Boards or ICSE) systems of evaluation and even with course contents. Despite this, a student who gets 75 per cent is unquestionably good. How come he or she is wandering around in desperation, not able to get admission? How come there are capitation fees? Capitation fees are nothing but bribes and this kind of bribe is only paid when there is shortage. Now that telephone connections are easily available, all associated bribes have disappeared. Therefore, the answer to capitation fees is not court intervention, but removal of shortages. And remember what I just said, there is no overall shortage. There is shortage of good quality educational institutions, which is where all the capitation fees are. How come more than 74,000 Indian students are headed for the United States? India is the largest exporter of students to the US now, having overtaken China. Notice that these students aren't always graduates. There is a sizeable chunk of under-graduates also. Aid is difficult at the under-graduate level. So these are students who often finance their own education, having failed to secure admission in good quality educational institutes in India.

How will you ensure good quality watches at affordable prices are produced in India? There was a day and age when we thought this could only be done through the public sector. There was also a day and age when we thought we should monitor costs and prices charged by private companies for everything under the sun. Thankfully, for manufacturing, we now appreciate that such attempts are dysfunctional and competition and market forces are enough. How is watch production different from providing educational services? Why should we then not throw open higher education to the private sector? You will argue that higher education is already open to the private sector. Not quite. It will be truly open if we stop trying to regulate tuition fees and faculty salaries. Other than court intervention, that's precisely what UGC and AICTE Acts try to do. Ditto for universities set up outside the UGC framework. Haven't we given up the idea of trying to regulate salaries of management? Why should there be centrally determined pay scales for teachers? Depending on performance and expertise, shouldn't a college or university have the freedom to contractually decide what it decides to pay a faculty member? This is a principle we generally accept. What is special about higher education that we must deviate from common sense?

Let's therefore thrown open higher education to the private sector in the true sense of the term and this should include the foreign private sector. We don't need entry barriers like recognition from UGC or AICTE. Today, students who head for the US (or elsewhere abroad) belong to the better-off sections of society who can afford loans or family finance. Isn't it better to broad-base this access by allowing better foreign institutions to function in India? As things stand, the shady ones are already here and students, who don't know any better, seek admission there. If you are with me so far, let me upset you by arguing I don't think we need to look upon education as a non-profit making exercise.

Many counter arguments advanced against private sector entry are false. Market-determined tuition fees don't mean the poor will be deprived access. Globally, private universities have scholarships that cross-subsidize the poor. After all, to establish credibility, the private sector also needs to attract good students, irrespective of means. Loans are possible. In general, the private sector also has lower administrative costs. If we want, we can also have government-financed scholarship schemes for the poor. This is a different proposition from arguing that tuition fees should be low for everyone.

Nor does private sector entry imply end of regulation. However, regulation is distinct from control. For instance, there should be clear disclosure norms for all institutions of higher education. Where does the money come from? What is it spent on? What is the educational background of students? What is the placement record? We do have problems with what balance sheets actually reveal. Subject to this caveat, this is a bit like arguing that educational institutes must have proper annual reports and balance sheets. This is important because education is one sector where there is asymmetry of information. With such mandatory disclosure, external agencies (not UGC or AICTE or other government agencies) can begin to rate educational institutions. There are indeed such attempts, usually by magazines. But those aren't exhaustive, and in the absence of complete disclosure, are also incomplete. Eventually, we will also probably have centralized exit exams like SAT or GRE and these records will also enable students and parents to judge institutions. Competition law has clauses on unfair trade practices. These too must be applicable to education, with efficient redressal mechanisms. Regulation will take care of the Chhattisgarh kind of problem.

In future, those 74,000 students should stay in India and we don't want suicides after IIT entrance results are out.

35

Health and Infrastructure

JUST as the State has a role in providing school education, the State also has a role to play in providing health care. I have said that the decade of the 1990s show some improvements in educational indicators. That hasn't yet happened for health. In 2000, the UN General Assembly adopted some goals known as the Millenium Development Goals (MDGs). These were targets to be attained by 2015. There are several MDGs, concerning poverty, hunger, education, health and gender disparities. India seems to be on track for attaining some of these goals. But certainly not on health. Not if we extrapolate present trends.

There are different indicators to judge health outcomes. Life expectancy at birth is one. Human Development Report (HDR) tells us that life expectancy at birth was 50.3 years in India between 1970 and 1975. Between 2000 and 2005, it will become 63.9 years. There has been improvement. The question is, has there been enough improvement, especially in comparison to other countries? And all-India figures are not necessarily the right ones. Because there are geographical differences and gender disparities. The National Human Development Report (NHDR) gives figures for the 1992 to 1996 period. While the all-India life expectancy is 60.7 years according to these figures, that in Madhya Pradesh is only 55.2 years.

The most common indicator of health outcomes is probably the infant mortality rate (IMR), expressed as the number of infant deaths per thousand births. In 1970, the IMR was 127. Now, it is around 67. But in MP or Orissa, the IMR continues to be almost 100. More importantly, declines in IMR seem to have slowed. In 1981, the IMR was 110 and in 1991, declined to 80. In 1996, it dropped to 72. But in 2001, it only dropped to 67. The under-five mortality rate is still 93 per thousand. The maternal mortality rate is still 540 per 100,000. 47 per cent of children are under-weight. Only 56 per cent of children are immunized against measles. Only 73 per cent of children are immunized against tuberculosis. Had UP not existed, polio would have vanished from the face of the earth. And it is impossible to quantify the adverse impact of morbidity.

Health - Inadequate Progress

Infant Mortality Rate

☐ 1951   ▨ 1971   ▩ 1981   ▨ 1991   ▨ 2000

Source: Economic Survey of India, various years

0.9 per cent of GDP is spent on health. This is public expenditure. The total expenditure on health is 5.2 per cent of GDP, the remainder coming from private expenditure. Despite possibilities of competition, health is not something that can be completely left to the private sector. What is worrying is that public expenditure on health is declining. Not very long ago, it used to be 1.3 per cent of GDP. The problem is of course the state of government finances. We need to increase public expenditure on health to at least 2 per cent of GDP. Remember of course that much of health is a State government subject. NHDR figures tell us how State government expenditure on health has also declined as a percentage of SDP (State domestic product). We get back to the reform question of opportunity costs. If money is being spent on unproductive government expenditure, where are the resources for spending on health? Besides, the efficiency of public expenditure on health is also a question mark. 75 per cent goes on salaries and pensions.

The preventive aspects of health care are also important. By that, I mean drinking water, sanitation, sewage treatment, immunization, food. We get back to the question of efficiency of government expenditure, its transparency and its accountability. Remember what I said in the context of education. Studies by Samuel Paul at the Public Affairs Centre in Bangalore and the Administrative Staff College in Hyderabad show that the poor are prepared to pay higher prices, provided service improves.

Health is social infrastructure. But similar points crop up about physical infrastructure also. Physical infrastructure means different things to different people. We can include power, telecom, roads, railways, aviation, airports, ports and even urban municipal services. In many of these areas, private sector participation is possible. So are public-private partnerships. Many infrastructure services can be unbundled. But it is equally true that in many infrastructure areas, public sector participation, through financing if not through providing, is inevitable. Has Indian infrastructure improved? Very selectively. There is telecom. There is civil aviation. Notwithstanding the National Highway Development Programme (NHDP) and the Pradhan Mantri Gram Sadak Yojana, road connectivity hasn't improved dramatically. And power availability has often deteriorated in many States. I mentioned the pro-rich and anti-poor perception of reforms earlier. This is partly due to what has happened, and what has not happened, in infrastructure. If improvements are witnessed in telecom and civil aviation, that is naturally perceived to be pro-rich. Had improvements in roads, water supply and power immediately taken place, this perception may well have been corrected.

Regardless of what is produced, regardless of whether it is produced in the public sector or the private sector, production will not be commercially viable as long as the cost of production is not recovered. And one problem with infrastructure reform is this question of appropriate user charges. To repeat the argument encountered earlier, there is no problem if we want to subsidize the poor. But how can the country afford to subsidize everyone? Understandably, those who have received infrastructure services free so far, refuse to pay for them now. On an average, in electricity distribution, so-called transmission and distribution (T&D) losses are as high as 40 per cent, although they should be no higher than 10 per cent. In a budget speech, a Finance Minister referred to T&D losses as theft and dacoity. As indeed they are. Rich farmers in Punjab and rich industrialists in Delhi steal power. Or pay nothing for it. Remember also that if you impose an artificially low price, you encourage over-use of that resource. Be it power or be it water.

At a certain level, this debate about privatizing infrastructure is a pointless one. For the poor, infrastructure services are already privatized. There is no public water supply. Water is only available from private water tankers and the poor pay much more for water than we do. Ditto for power and ditto for many other infrastructure services. Sometimes, the poor pay by not obtaining these services at all. If we extrapolate present trends, it will take 226 years for all of undivided Bihar to be electrified. In the former Soviet Union, Lenin defined socialism as electrification plus the Soviets. We have had the Soviets, but not the electrification. A most perverse definition of socialism.

36

Taxes

TO do the kinds of things we want the government to do, the government needs money. In general, this has to come through taxes. There is some kind of tax fatigue in India. Let me explain what I mean by this. But before that, let me point out that there is a difference between a tax and a fee. At least, legally. A fee is paid for a specific service. There is a clear quid pro quo. So if I don't get the services from the government, assuming the government is the provider, I can take the government to task. A tax is not like that. There is no quid pro quo. I have no means of checking what the money collected through taxes is going to be used for. And because I am skeptical of the use being made by the government of tax money and also skeptical about the Parliamentary scrutiny, as a citizen, I am reluctant to pay taxes. The tax/GDP ratio in India is 9.6 per cent. It has actually declined since 1990-91, when it used to be 10.1 per cent. If we want the government to do the various things we want it to do, the tax/GDP ratio has to increase. Perhaps even to 15 per cent of GDP.

There were two sensible Kelkar Task Force reports on direct and indirect taxes. With sensible recommendations that have now gone for a six. Take these proposals one at a time.

What is the popular impression? Salaried employees have no option. They bear the brunt of taxation. The non-salaried evade taxes. Look at businessmen (or women), lawyers and doctors. But let's be a bit careful about what we mean by evasion. Do we mean that such people don't submit income tax returns or do we mean that having submitted income tax returns, they don't disclose their right income? There is a difference. Thanks to the 1/6 scheme, which is expanding, I don't think the former is an issue. Look at it this way. How many households are there in India? Probably around 200 million. Today, agricultural income, including non-agricultural income of farmers, is outside the tax net. That probably leaves around 65 million urban households. Almost 30 million already submit income tax returns. Given exemption limits, this number is unlikely to increase significantly. The problem thus is with under-declaration, rather than with non-submission of returns. How do we remove under-declaration? I don't see what is wrong with PAN becoming something like a social security number. Nor do I see what is wrong with PAN numbers being mandatory for several transactions. This is the TIN (Tax Information Network) idea. Apart from reasonable rates, that's the best way to check under-declaration. Left to the Income Tax department, we should indeed be skeptical about whether TIN will ever take off. Hence the argument about outsourcing. I don't see why people should object to that. The related procedural improvements should also be universally welcomed. And as long as exemptions continue, there is no way we will be able to check under-declaration of income.

Honestly, why shouldn't farmers pay income taxes? Two-thirds of consumption takes place in rural India. NCAER studies show that two-thirds of the filthy rich (this is not a NCAER expression though) are also in rural India. No one is asking poor farmers to pay income taxes. After all, there is a threshold. As far as I know, no one has questioned the Task Force's figure that given a threshold of 1 lakh, 95 per cent of farmers will be exempted. States don't have the guts to tax agricultural income. The Article 252 proposal, requiring support of at least two States, doesn't seem a bad one at all. That way, States get to keep the revenue (net of collection costs) and this eases their fiscal pressures. But they also get the Centre to carry the can. This seems more feasible than the alternative proposal of empowering *panchayats* to tax farm income. We are now left with the proposals on personal and corporate income taxation.

There seem to be two kinds of arguments against personal income tax proposals. First, exemptions are going. Second, the burden on income tax payers will increase. Isn't it true that exemptions are inherently discretionary and distort resource allocation? Take savings. Why should we try to artificially encourage savings and what is the definition of savings? Ask the so-called common man in the street about the form in which he (or she) keeps his savings. Gold and real estate will figure. The former is actually treated as consumption and the latter is not rewarded through exemptions. The exemption-based reward is for financial savings and the government needs to pre-empt these resources to sustain inordinately high fiscal deficits. After pre-emption, precious little is left for investments, which is the reason we want to reward savings in the first place. And what is the definition of investments? If we reward investments in physical capital, we automatically assume investments in human capital should not be so rewarded. This is in additional to complexities across different saving instruments. Nor will the argument about lack of social safety nets entirely wash. Social safety nets are indeed necessary. But who needs them more? 30 million income tax assessees, or the 173 million who don't submit returns? Since there are no free lunches, rewarding the former (in any form) comes at the expense of the latter and that is regressive.

Therefore, I think the Kelkar Task Force's recommendations on direct taxes should immediately be adopted. Notwithstanding what Rajnath Singh thought. Which leaves indirect taxes. Indirect taxes have an import duty angle and a domestic angle. Let me ignore customs duties. I have said enough about customs duties earlier. On domestic indirect taxes, the present system is non-transparent and inefficient. It has cost cascading effects, what with excise, central sales tax, State-level sales taxes and local body taxes like octroi. It makes it difficult for us to defend ourselves against anti-dumping and anti-subsidy investigations abroad. It makes it impossible for Commerce Ministry to work out a system of WTO-compliant export incentives. We should all want a transition to a complete VAT (value added tax), with no exemptions and procedural simplifications. And with service sector taxation that is properly integrated into VAT. That's a long way off. But even the limited movement towards VAT has been postponed. Even though the States agreed. Traders who evade taxes don't want VAT. We want the evasion. But we want the government to do various things for us. That's a most peculiar argument and the only ones who suffer are the poor.

37

The Golden BRIC Road

THE BRIC report has sometimes been quoted in Indian papers, but not in great detail. Anyone with an interest in the Indian economy should read the BRIC report. You will find it readily on the Net. More accurately, the BRIC report is Global Economics Paper No. 99, brought out by Goldman Sachs in October 2003 and is titled, "Dreaming with BRICs: The Path to 2050". BRIC stands for Brazil, Russia, India and China.

Here are the startling facts for BRICs as a group. In less than 40 years, the BRIC economies can together be larger than the G-6 (US, Japan, Germany, France, Italy, UK) in dollar terms. These are also real dollars, or if you like, today's dollars. Of the current G-6, only US and Japan will be among the six largest economies in the world in 2050. About two-thirds of the increase in GDP from the BRICs will come from higher real growth. The balance will be through currency appreciation and BRIC exchange rates may appreciate at an average rate of 2.5 per cent a year. As early as 2009, the annual increase in US dollar spending from the BRICs can be greater than that from the G6. By 2025 the annual increase in US dollar spending from the BRICs can be twice that of the G6, and four times higher by 2050.

The shift in GDP relative to the G6 takes place steadily over the period, but is most dramatic in the first 30 years. In 30 years, India's economy is likely to be the third largest in the world, after US and China. Growth for the BRICs is likely to slow significantly towards the end of the period, with only India seeing growth rates significantly above 3 per cent by 2050. But individuals in the BRICs are still likely to be poorer on average than individuals in the G6 economies, with the exception of Russia. That is, even after the growth, per capita income in BRICs will be lower than in G-6.

Okay, there is some skepticism about what Goldman Sachs have to say on Brazil and Russia. But I don't think there can be too much skepticism about the Indian projections. Several people have done projections for India, although these projections are usually up to 2020, not 2050. The Tenth Plan (2002-07) talks about 8 per cent GDP growth. Even if 8 per cent isn't likely, most people will accept 7 per cent as an acceptable trend over the next 20 years. However, unlike Goldman Sachs, most economists don't usually factor in demographic transition in such projections. Let's state it simply. Fewer babies are being born in India now. At least at an all-India level. But several babies were born 20 or 25 years ago and those babies are now entering the labour force. This reduces the dependency ratio. Of course, productivity of these new entrants depends on whether they have education and skills and whether jobs can be found for them. East Asia went through this demographic transition 20 to 30 years ago and econometric estimates suggest this demographic transition added a clear 2 per cent to GDP growth in East Asia. Even if we don't get an increment of 2 per cent, why should we not get an increment of at least 1 per cent thanks to demographic transition? Today, the rate of population growth is around 1.8 per cent and should slow down to 1.5 per cent in the next 10 years and perhaps 1.3 per cent in the subsequent 10 years. If you take away 1.5 per cent from 7 per cent, you still get 5.5 per cent per capita GDP growth. In other words, 5.5 per cent is perfectly reasonable.

Compare this 5.5 per cent with what Goldman Sachs have, broken up into a productivity gains contribution and a demo-graphic component. The assumed per capita GDP growth is 3.7 per cent for 2000-05, 7.5 per cent for 2005-10, 7.4 per cent for 2010-15, 7.2 per cent for 2015-20, 7.4 per cent for 2020-25, 8.2 per cent for 2025-30, 8.9 per cent for 2030-35, 8.9 per cent for 2035-40, 8.3 per cent for 2040-45 and 7.6 per cent for 2045-50. You get such precise numbers because they come out of a model. The difference with traditional economic forecasting is that no economist normally dares to forecast or predict exchange rate behavior. Hence, if you find an economist juggling around with that 5.5 per cent per capita, that growth will be applied on today's base per capita income of say 500 US dollars, assuming the exchange rate stays unchanged. Goldman Sachs convincingly argue that with growth, there will be capital inflows and with capital inflows, the rupee has to appreciate. Remember that average appreciation of 2.5 per cent a year. Since per capita income is a rupee figure, any rupee appreciation vis-à-vis the US dollar, results in a higher dollar per capita income figure. Think of it slightly differently. Before the reforms started, the rupee's exchange rate vis-à-vis the dollar was around 21 rupees. Today, it is around 45 rupees. Had the exchange rate continued to be 21 rupees to a dollar, the Indian per capita income today would have been around 1070 dollars, not 500. Goldman Sachs rightly argue that as economies develop, you can't mess around with the exchange rate. It attains its true value. Part of the reason (roughly one-third of the reason) why Goldman Sachs get higher per capita growths than other projections is because of this exchange rate appreciation. As I said earlier, you will find the detailed assumptions in the model, in the paper that is freely available on the Internet. But to me, the assumptions seem to be perfectly realistic. Not best-case scenarios. But most-likely scenarios.

What kind of dollar per capita incomes do these growths translate to? 468 dollars in 2000, 559 in 2005, 804 in 2010, 1149 in 2015, 1622 in 2020, 2331 in 2025, 3473 in 2030, 5327 in 2035, 8124 in 2040, 12046 in 2045 and 17386 in 2050. The mind begins to boggle because these are stretched to beyond 2020. Several people have talked about around 1500 in 2020 and no one has batted an eyelid. It becomes easier to appreciate these numbers if we link them to where other countries are today. In 2010, we will be roughly where Ukraine is today. In 2015, we will be roughly where Paraguay is today. In 2020, we will be roughly where Iran is today. In 2025, we will be roughly where the Dominican Republic is today. In 2030, we will be roughly where Latvia is today. In 2035, we will be roughly where Hungary is today. In 2040, we will be roughly where South Korea is today. In 2045, we will be roughly where Greece is today. And in 2050, we will be roughly where Italy is today. Remember that we have an enormous amount of catching up to do.

That per capita income of 17386 dollars in 2050 may make us salivate. But in 2050, Brazil will have a per capita income of 26592, China of 31357, Russia of 49646, France of 51594, Germany of 48952, Italy of 40901, Japan of 66805, UK of 59122 and US of 83710. To me, the importance of these numbers lies elsewhere. After all, per capita income is only a means. It is not the end product. To me, improvements in human development indicators are much more important. That's when a country becomes "developed" and that is not something the present Goldman Sachs report is interested in. But using these figures, I can hazard a guess that we are looking at around 2042, when the per capita income threshold of 10,000 dollars is crossed. Certainly not in 2020.

38

Postscript – Redeeming the Pledge

ON several occasions, in this book, I have argued the following. India is a poor country, whether we like it or not. Today, India's per capita income is 500 US dollars. The richest country in the world has a per capita income of 50,000 US dollars. A large percentage of India's population lives below the poverty line. Indicators like life expectancy or infant mortality are also far worse than what they should be.

To change this, growth is needed. That's the logic of reforms. Inject competition. Competition drives efficiency. Efficiency drives growth. Indeed, in the 1990s, the Indian economy grew at an annual average real rate of around 6.5 per cent. That is not good enough. The Tenth Plan (2002-07) still talks of 8 per cent, although that looks increasingly elusive. Growth at around 6.5 per cent takes the Indian per capita income to around 1500 US dollars in 2020, in today's dollars. That doesn't make India a developed economy, using the standard definition of developed. Nor does it catapult India into the high human development category.

Having said that, clearly perceptions about India are changing and there are several reasons for this. First, the 1990s have been associated with several successes in the external sector, including software exports, the current account surplus and burgeoning foreign exchange reserves. Second, the rate of population growth is slowly down at an all-India level (although there are inter-regional variations) and this implies a higher per capita income growth, with consequent explosion in consumption. A decrease in the dependency ratio also stimulates income growth and demographically, India is probably poised today where several East Asian economies were poised in the 1960s. Third, educational indicators have begun to improve. Subject to inter-regional variations, increase in literacy from 52 per cent in 1991 to 65 per cent in 2001 is one manifestation of this. This now needs to be replicated for health outcomes. Fourth, food stocks are spilling over, although this is not always an unmitigated plus. Fifth, Indian companies have become leaner and more competitive. While not everyone can survive in an atmosphere of competition, the ones that have survived are efficient and can handle global competition. Finally, transcending all the above points, India has begun to be noticed globally. IT, H1-B visas, success of Indian professionals (or those of Indian origin) based in the United States, business process out-sourcing and call centres are all manifestations. One instance of changing perceptions about India is in the BRIC report.

But make no mistake. Despite the euphoria about 2020, India in 2020 will be more or less where China is today. If the explosion takes place, that will take place later. And whether it is 2020 or 2050, we need the reforms to get going.

The agenda of reforms has been pending for a long time, now described as second generation reforms. I have mentioned this domestic reform agenda earlier, but have never spelt it out. So here it is. In this agenda, one should mention rural sector reforms, infrastructure, direct and indirect taxes, legal reform, the small-scale sector, targeting of subsidies, downsizing and making government more accountable and public sector reform. *Per se*, the fiscal deficit should not be mentioned as a separate problem. While the fiscal deficit is indeed high, and the composition of the fiscal deficit is such that it is driven by revenue rather than capital expenditure, this problem cannot be addressed unless one solves the issue of interest payments, defence expenditure and subsidies. In other words, the fiscal deficit problem will automatically be addressed once the other reforms take place. And in the absence of a consensus on those reforms, saying that there is a consensus on reducing the fiscal deficit (or the revenue deficit) is neither here nor there. The fact that there is no consensus on a minimum common set of reforms has been repeated ad nauseam. Perhaps the consensus becomes easier to generate if the liberalization package is specifically linked to an explicitly articulated economic goal. That is, the roadmap emerges from the goal. Despite more than a decade of economic reforms, this attempt hasn't yet taken place.

Nor can we forget the issue of relatively disadvantaged sections. One cannot forget that 26 per cent of the Indian population is poor. That amounts to 300 million households. Quite often, these poor households are located in certain specified districts in States like undivided Bihar, undivided Madhya Pradesh, Rajasthan, undivided Uttar Pradesh, Maharashtra, Karnataka, Andhra Pradesh, Orissa, West Bengal and the North-East. These are pockets of deprivation. Arguably, the decade of the 1990s has increased inter-regional disparities and these populations and these geographical areas have been bypassed and marginalized by the trickle down benefits of growth. The national goal cannot be accepted as a national one without a buy-in by these deprived sections. Nor can the State abdicate from the responsibility of providing (or at least financing) a whole variety of social and physical infrastructure, including subsidizing households that are below the poverty line (BPL). In other words, the national goal should also have objectives like the following. Increase the literacy rate to 80 per cent and the gross enrolment ratio to 80 per cent by 2010.

Reduce the infant mortality rate to 30 by 2010. These are precise goals and concrete deadlines people can identify with. Vague assertions like India becoming a developed economy will not do.

I suspect that we still lack the confidence to realize that India has changed and India can take on the world. I suspect this has something to do with the age profiles of people who formulate policy. I suspect we need a confident younger generation to take over policy formulation, a generation that was bred, and perhaps even born, in the decade of the 1990s, in the decade of the satellite and assorted other revolutions. That generation will demand second generation and perhaps even third generation reforms and even implement them. At a facile level, if you try to work out when this generation will come of age to demand policy changes, you will arrive at a year around 2015. More or less the year when a generation born after Independence will begin to formulate policy. After all, policy formulation in India is left to those who are plus 65 years of age.

In the altered global environment, power flows out of the barrel of economics rather than politics. The national identity needs to be forged around an intended economic tryst. That's the noble mansion of free India we can strive towards. Where the pledge is concrete enough to be met in full measure. Not partly or very substantially.

More generally, there were times when one almost felt ashamed of being an Indian. There is now the promise that this might change. Too early yet to feel proud. But the promise is there.

꩜ ꩜